cupcakes

Luscious bakeshop favorites from your home kitchen

recipes by Shelly Kaldunski

photographs by David Matheson

A Fireside Book
Published by Simon & Schuster
New York   London   Toronto   Sydney

Contents

All About Cupcakes

Once upon a time, cupcakes were treats just for kids. With colorful sprinkles and bright, brassy decorations, cupcakes were meant to enchant the youthful eye, and the sugary cake and frosting were made to tickle kids' insatiable sweet tooth. What's more, cupcakes didn't—and still don't—require the formality of a fork to eat and they're baked in pint-sized portions so no sharing is ever required. As a kid, what's *not* to love about cupcakes?

But at long last, adults have begun to realize what they've been missing and cupcakes' popularity has soared. Chic, stylish cupcakes can be found in boutique bakeries, on trendy A-list restaurant menus, and even at fashionable nuptials. There's no rule that says it's necessary to have a special occasion to enjoy cupcakes. Packed into a lunchbox as a surprise for an unsuspecting student, dished up as a weeknight dessert, or served to friends after a casual supper, cupcakes are welcome little indulgences at any time.

In this book, you will find cupcake recipes for every palate. For traditionalists there are Yellow Cupcakes (page 24) with Chocolate Buttercream (page 105). There are riffs on classic desserts, such as Black Forest Cupcakes (page 67) and Tiramisu Cupcakes (page 87). For discerning adult taste buds, there are Chai & Honey Cupcakes (page 34) and Salted Caramel Cupcakes (page 85). Kids will love PB & J Cupcakes (page 60) and Rocky Road Cupcakes (page 79). And, of course, you will find ideas for decorating your cupcakes with modern minimalism, elegant flourishes, and colorful exuberance.

NAME THAT CUPCAKE

Two theories exist about how cupcakes came to be called cupcakes. One theory supposes that they got their name because they were baked in small cups or tea cups to create individually sized cakes. The other theorizes that cupcakes, like pound cakes, were named after the formula or recipe that was used to make them: one cup each of butter, sugar, flour, and eggs.

Ingredients

BUTTER There's nothing like the richness of pure butter in baked goods. For cupcakes and frostings, be sure that the butter you use is unsalted. Unsalted butter allows you to have full control over the amount of salt that goes into a recipe. On the package, unsalted butter is sometimes labeled as "sweet" butter. For the best results, do not use butter substitutes: In addition to affecting flavor, butter substitutes may also affect the cupcakes' texture.

FLOUR There are two types of flour commonly used in cake making: all-purpose flour and cake flour. All-purpose flour has a higher protein content than cake flour and, by comparison, yields a firmer cake texture. Cake flour is often used in recipes when a plush, ultra-tender cake texture is desired. If cake flour is not available, for every 1 cup of cake flour needed, use ⅞ cup (¾ cup plus 2 tablespoons) all-purpose flour plus 2 tablespoons cornstarch.

SUGARS Sugar gives cupcakes their sweetness. It also tenderizes, adds moisture, and promotes browning during baking. Granulated sugar is the kind most often used in baking because it has a neutral flavor. Brown sugar contains molasses, which makes it moist and gives it caramel-like nuances. It's great for use in recipes that contain assertive flavors. Confectioners' sugar, also called powdered sugar, is granulated sugar that has been pulverized to a fine powder and combined with cornstarch. Confectioners' sugar is often used in glazes, frostings, and for dusting sweets just before serving.

EGGS The recipes in this book, like most others, were developed with large eggs. If the eggs need to be separated, it's easier to do so when they're cold and the yolks are firm. If you'll be whipping the egg whites, they must be free of bits of yolk and fat, so use care when separating the eggs, and be sure that the bowl and beaters that you use to whip the whites are clean.

BAKING SODA AND BAKING POWDER Baking soda and baking powder are leavening agents that help cupcake batter rise during baking. Baking soda is used when the batter contains an acidic ingredient like buttermilk or sour cream. Baking powder can be used in the presence or absence of an acidic ingredient. Before using an already-opened container of baking powder, check the expiration date and replace it if it's expired, as old baking powder often does not provide proper lift.

Equipment

ELECTRIC MIXER An electric mixer is a kitchen workhorse for bakers. Many cupcake batters can be made without one, but for most types of frosting, an electric mixer is an important piece of equipment. A standing mixer is more efficient than a hand mixer because it leaves the baker's hands free to do other tasks, and it has a motor that can power through heavy batters and frostings. The recipes in this book were developed using a standing mixer.

CUPCAKE LINERS Cupcake liners are available in solid colors, prints, pastel hues, bold tones, and made of shiny foils. If the muffin pan is well greased, it's not necessary to use cupcake liners, but liners ensure effortless removal from the muffin pan, and make it easy to handle the cupcakes when frosting them. They also make clean-up a snap. Some of the filled cupcakes in this book were developed without cupcake liners.

MUFFIN PANS Standard muffin pans have twelve cups, each with a ½-cup capacity. Jumbo muffin pans have six cups of ¾-cup capacity. Mini muffin pans have twenty-four tiny cups that hold about 3 tablespoons apiece. Most of the cupcakes in this book are baked in standard muffin pans, with just a handful baked in jumbo or mini muffin pans.

FOOD COLORING
Standard liquid food coloring from the supermarket comes in very basic colors that can be combined to create other colors. Food coloring pastes and gels are sold in specialty stores, and come in a wide array of colors so that mixing is unnecessary. These pastes are very highly concentrated so only tiny amounts are needed—for example, to tint a buttercream, dip the tip of a paring knife into the paste and stir in the color. Keep in mind that subtle hues are more appealing than bright ones, and that color can always be added, but it cannot be subtracted.

If you're baking a double batch of cupcakes, it's best to make and bake the batches one at a time rather than double the recipe and bake them all at once. Doubling-up in the oven interferes with heat circulation and can cause the cupcakes to bake and rise unevenly. However, if you leave half of a doubled batch of batter to stand while the first half bakes, the leavener will begin to activate before baking begins, and the result may be dense, squat cupcakes. By making and baking one batch of cupcakes at a time, you're assured perfect cupcakes every time.

ICE CREAM SCOOP Thin, pourable batters are easy to divide between muffin pan cups, but for thick, heavy batters, an ice cream scoop—in particular, a spring-loaded ice cream scoop—comes in handy. With a spring-loaded scoop, you can easily measure out the batter and drop it cleanly into the muffin pan cups with just the press of the thumb.

SILICONE SPATULA Silicone spatulas are indispensable kitchen tools. With wide, flexible blades, silicone spatulas scrape out every last bit from the bowl and easily smooth over the batter's surface. Unlike rubber spatulas, silicone spatulas are heat- and stain-resistant, and resist picking up food odors. They're available in a range of sizes—having a large, medium, and small silicone spatula ensures that you have one suited to any baking or cooking task.

Making and baking the batter

When making cupcake batter, the temperature of the ingredients is important. Butter that's cold and hard is difficult to beat with a mixer, and cold eggs are difficult to incorporate. Before beginning, read through the recipe to see which refrigerated ingredients need to be brought to room temperature. In a pinch, you can soften butter in a microwave (use low power and 5- to 10-second increments), and you can remove the chill from cold eggs by submerging them in a bowl of tepid water for a few minutes. Before you begin mixing, have all your ingredients measured and ready so that you will not need to stop to rummage through the cupboard. Many batters are made with an electric mixer. Others are made by hand with only a whisk or wooden spoon. Those cupcakes that are lightened with whipped egg whites have the whites gently folded in right at the end. No matter the mixing method, once the wet and dry ingredients are in the bowl together,

use a light hand and mix the batter only until it is just combined. Overmixing can result in tough, chewy cupcakes.

Cupcakes bake best in the center of the oven. If your oven heats unevenly or has hot spots, rotate the muffin pan—very gently so as not the deflate the cupcakes—midway through baking to ensure that the cupcakes rise and brown evenly. To test the doneness of most unfilled cupcakes, insert a toothpick or skewer into the center of one of the cupcakes. If it comes out clean, the cupcakes are done.

Filling and frosting your cupcakes

A filling adds a luscious, extra-special touch to a simple cupcake. Some cupcakes, such as the Black and White Cupcakes (page 76), have a filling that's baked right in; others, such as the Coconut-Lime Cupcakes (page 55) are filled after baking and cooling. The decision to fill before or after baking is often determined by the type of filling—sturdy cream cheese can stand up to baking, but delicate citrus curd cannot.

When you frost your cupcakes, make sure that the icing is soft and spreadable. If you're using a buttercream, the buttercream should be at room temperature. Frosting cupcakes can be as simple as spreading frosting with a butter knife or as involved as piping it with a pastry bag and tip. Peaks, swooshes, and swirls of frosting add texture, volume, and a whimsical touch; a smooth coat of glossy glaze lends a sleek, sophisticated look. For a polished look, you can sprinkle or decorate the frosted cupcakes with embellishments such as shredded coconut (toasted or untoasted), chopped nuts, fresh berries, candied citrus peel, sugared edible flowers, chocolate curls and shavings, or colored sugars, to name just a few ideas.

FILLING A PASTRY BAG

If you're using a pastry bag to pipe frosting onto your cupcakes, select a bag that holds enough frosting so that you won't need to refill it repeatedly (for cupcakes, a 14- or 16-inch bag is a good size). Fit the pastry bag with the pastry tip, then fold back the top 3–4 inches of the bag to form a cuff. Scoop the frosting into the bag, filling it about two-thirds full, and unfold the cuff. Gather and then twist the top of the bag, pushing the frosting toward the tip, until a spot of frosting comes out and any air bubbles near the tip of the pastry bag have been released.

Preparing cupcakes for filling and frosting

Cupcakes are just plain little cakes until they're filled or frosted, or, better yet, both filled and frosted. Before embellishing with a filling or frosting, make sure that your cupcakes have cooled completely to room temperature. Warm cupcakes are very delicate in texture, making them riskier to handle, and the slightest amount of heat can soften or melt the filling or frosting.

COOLING   Before filling or frosting your cupcakes, make sure that they are completely cooled so that they don't melt the filling or frosting. Whether in or out of the muffin pan, the best way to cool your cupcakes is on a wire rack, which allows air to circulate all around them so that they cool in the minimum amount of time.

SPLITTING   To split a cupcake into layers for sandwiching a filling, use a paring knife and cut the cupcake in half horizontally. Use a gentle sawing motion, holding the knife parallel to the work surface so that the cut is perfectly level. For the best appearance, match the cupcake tops with their respective bottoms.

HOLLOWING   A cupcake may be hollowed or cored to create a space for filling. Using a paring knife inserted at an angle and a gentle sawing motion, rotate the cupcake, trimming out a cone-shaped piece about 1½ inches in diameter and about 1 inch deep. Discard the cores or keep them for nibbling.

Basic frosting techniques

Frosting a cupcake is as simple or as involved as you make it. The easiest way is with a casual pouf of frosting. Creating peaks and swirls in the frosting gives the cupcakes a fun and carefree feel; a smooth coat gives them a more elegant and refined look. No special or hard-to-use tools are required, just an item or two that you may already have stashed in your kitchen drawer.

ICING SPATULA   A small icing spatula with a 4-inch blade is ideal for frosting cupcakes. Dollop a generous amount of frosting onto the center of the cupcake, then use the spatula to spread it. The spatula's round tip is good for creating swirls in the frosting, and its thin, flat blade also excels at creating smooth surfaces.

SPOON   A spoon is a useful tool for frosting cupcakes. Choose one that is shallow and wide, with a rounded tip, if possible. Drop a spoonful of frosting onto the center of the cupcake, then, with the back of the spoon, spread the frosting. Use the backside of the tip of the spoon to create swooshes and swirls.

ICE CREAM SCOOP   A spring-loaded ice cream scoop is a quick and easy way to top a cupcake with frosting. Use a scoop about 2 inches in diameter to place a dome of frosting on the cupcake. Then, gently press the back of the scoop into the frosting to flatten it slightly and push it out to the edges of the cupcake.

Basic piping techniques

Even the novice cupcake decorator can create boutique-bakery cupcakes with a pastry bag and tip. Get a little practice by piping designs onto a clean plate. When you're ready to start decorating, the practice frosting can be put back into the pastry bag and reused. Buttercreams and cream cheese frosting are the most forgiving types of frosting to use for creating piped designs.

PLAIN TIP   A spiral of frosting, made with a large plain tip, is a clean, simple design. Start at the center of the cupcake and, applying even pressure to the pastry bag, move the tip in a spiral motion, working outward to the edge of the cupcake, then build upward, still moving in a spiral motion and piling the frosting on top of itself. Finish at the center of the cupcake.

CLOSED STAR TIP   To create a decorative fluted swirl of frosting, use a pastry bag fitted with a large open star tip. Start on the outer edge of the cupcake, applying even pressure to the pastry bag, and work inward in a circular motion, overlapping the circles slightly and building upward, finishing at the center of the cupcake. Release pressure before pulling the tip away.

LEAF TIP   A large leaf tip can be used to create a ruffled ribbon-like effect. With the opening of the leaf tip held in a vertical position, pipe the frosting, applying even pressure to the pastry bag. Use a zigzag movement to move the tip in and out from the center of the cupcake to the edge. Rotate the cupcake as you pipe to cover the entire surface with frosting.

Fanciful piped designs

If you are comfortable using a pastry bag and have a few different types of pastry tips, there are many fanciful, yet simple, designs that can be piped onto your cupcakes. If you like, practice piping techniques and designs on a clean plate. When you're comfortable with the technique and ready to pipe directly onto the cupcakes, return the practice frosting to the pastry bag and reuse the frosting.

DOTS Use a pastry bag fitted with a large plain tip to pipe dots of frosting. Hold the pastry bag vertically, squeeze the bag to pipe a round dot, and release pressure before pulling the tip up and away. Begin piping around the edge of the cupcake. Build the dots up, staggering them slightly and working toward the center of the cupcake. Finish at the very center of the cupcake.

STARS To decorate the cupcake with tall pointed stars, use a large open star tip. Hold the pastry bag vertically, perpendicular to the surface of the cupcake. Squeeze the bag to pipe a star, then gradually release pressure on the pastry bag as you slowly lift the tip up and away from the cupcake. Continue in the same manner, piping until the cupcake is covered with stars.

RIBBONS Folded ribbons are made with a large basketweave tip. Hold the bag at a slight angle, with the fluted side up. In one continuous movement, begin piping at the upper third of the cupcake, near the center, pulling outward to the edge, then fold the frosting on itself; continue piping to the other edge and fold the frosting on itself, flipping the tip so that the fluted side is up.

Decorating with glazes

Glazes offer different decorating options and work best on cupcakes with flat tops. A layer of chocolate or vanilla glaze can be used alone or as a base for whimsical designs. If you'll be creating designs on the base, choose a contrasting color for the second glaze. Glazes are thinner in consistency than frostings, so a parchment paper cone is best for piping; otherwise, use a small pastry bag with a very fine writing tip.

POLKA DOTS To create polka dot cupcakes, simply pipe small dots of contrasting-colored glaze onto the glazed cupcakes. You can pipe same-sized dots in a fixed pattern or dots of different sizes using random placement. For dots of only one color, use only one glaze, or for playful multi-colored dots, use as many colored glazes as you like.

MONOGRAMS Pipe monograms onto glazed cupcakes to create personalized cupcakes. When piping monograms, exaggerated curls and swirls make plain lettering look grand and festive. (If you think you have an unsteady hand, practice first on a plate or baking sheet. Unlike frosting, piped glaze cannot be reused because it dries as it sits.)

SPIDER WEBS To make a spider web, pipe concentric circles onto a glazed cupcake. Lightly draw the tip of a wooden skewer, toothpick, or paring knife from the center of the cupcake outward to the edge, occasionally alternating the direction, if you choose. For the cleanest look, wipe the tip of the skewer after each draw.

Ideas for decorations and garnishes

Cupcakes can be decorated in countless ways—it simply takes a little imagination to come up with ideas for unique finishes that add color, texture, and artistry to your cupcakes. Depending on how much effort you would like to put into the finishing touches, decorations can be as simple as colorful candies or they can be as intricate as abstract caramel embellishments.

CANDIES   Use a pastry bag fitted with a small star tip to pipe petite stars or rosettes onto the cupcakes, then gently press colorful candies or decorations into the center of each. Pipe the stars or rosettes so that their size works well with the size of the candies that you plan to use, and, if you like, match the color of the candies to the occasion.

CHOCOLATE CURLS   To make chocolate curls, gently warm a block of chocolate by micro-waving it for 5–10 seconds at 75 percent power, then run a vegetable peeler along its length. The curls can be refrigerated for up to 1 week. Be sure to handle the chocolate curls with care because the heat of your hands will easily melt them.

CARAMEL DESIGNS   To make caramel garnishes, line a baking sheet with parchment paper or a nonstick baking mat. Cook 1 cup of sugar in a heavy saucepan over medium-high heat until amber in color. Working very carefully, use a spoon to drizzle the caramel in designs onto the prepared baking sheet. Let the caramel cool, then carefully peel off the pieces.

Basic Cupcakes

Vanilla Cupcakes

Vanilla cupcakes are the perfect base for myriad fillings and frostings. For the richest, fullest flavor and fragrance, use pure vanilla extract. Or, better yet, if you're willing to splurge, add the seeds from a vanilla bean to the batter along with the extract.

1¼ cups all-purpose flour

1½ tsp baking powder

¼ tsp salt

¾ cup sugar

6 tbsp unsalted butter, at room temperature

1 large egg, plus 1 large egg white, at room temperature

1 tsp vanilla extract

½ cup whole milk

Vanilla Buttercream (page 105)

Nonpareils and colored sugars for garnish, optional

MAKES 12 CUPCAKES

Position a rack in the middle of the oven and preheat to 350°F. Line a standard 12-cup muffin pan with paper or foil liners.

In a bowl, whisk together the flour, baking powder, and salt. In a large bowl, using an electric mixer on medium-high speed, beat the sugar and butter together until light and fluffy, 2–3 minutes. Add the egg and egg white one at a time, beating well on low speed after each addition, then beat in the vanilla. Add the flour mixture in 3 additions, alternating with the milk in 2 additions, beating on low speed until just combined; scrape down the sides of the bowl as needed. Beat on medium-high speed just until no traces of flour remain, about 30 seconds; do not overbeat.

Divide the batter evenly among the prepared muffin cups, filling each about three-fourths full. Bake until lightly golden and a toothpick inserted into the center of a cupcake comes out clean, 18–20 minutes. Let the cupcakes cool in the pan on a wire rack for 5 minutes. Transfer the cupcakes to the wire rack and let cool completely, about 1 hour.

Frost the cupcakes with the buttercream. (The frosted cupcakes can be refrigerated in an airtight container for up to 3 days; bring to room temperature before finishing.) Garnish the cupcakes with the colored sugars and nonpareils, if using, and serve.

Yellow Cupcakes

Rich, tender, buttery yellow cupcakes are always crowd pleasers. The classic pairing for yellow cupcakes is a smooth and silky chocolate buttercream, but, really, just about any flavor of frosting would be a good match.

1¼ cups all-purpose flour

1¼ tsp baking powder

¼ tsp salt

¾ cup sugar

6 tbsp unsalted butter, at room temperature

2 large eggs, at room temperature

1 tsp vanilla extract

⅓ cup whole milk

Chocolate Buttercream (page 105)

MAKES 12 CUPCAKES

Position a rack in the middle of the oven and preheat to 350°F. Line a standard 12-cup muffin pan with paper or foil liners.

In a bowl, whisk together the flour, baking powder, and salt. In another bowl, using an electric mixer on medium-high speed, beat the sugar and butter together until light and fluffy, 2–3 minutes. Add the eggs and vanilla and beat until combined. Add the flour mixture in 3 additions, alternating with the milk in 2 additions, beating on low speed until just combined; scrape down the sides of the bowl as needed. Beat on medium-high speed just until no traces of flour remain, about 30 seconds; do not overbeat.

Divide the batter evenly among the prepared muffin cups, filling each about three-fourths full. Bake until lightly golden and a toothpick inserted into the center of a cupcake comes out clean, 18–20 minutes. Let the cupcakes cool in the pan on a wire rack for 5 minutes. Transfer the cupcakes to the wire rack and let cool completely, about 1 hour.

Frost the cupcakes with the buttercream and serve. (The frosted cupcakes can be refrigerated in an airtight container for up to 3 days; bring to room temperature before serving.)

Chocolate Cupcakes

There are two secrets to these cupcakes. They get their rich, extra-chocolaty flavor from a combination of unsweetened cocoa powder and bittersweet chocolate, and their soft, moist texture from a simple hand-mixing method.

⅔ cup all-purpose flour

2½ tbsp unsweetened cocoa powder

¾ tsp baking powder

¼ tsp salt

3 oz bittersweet chocolate, chopped

½ cup plus 3 tbsp unsalted butter, cut into pieces

¾ cup plus 2 tbsp sugar

3 large eggs, at room temperature

1 tsp vanilla extract

Coffee, Chocolate, or Vanilla Buttercream (page 105)

Grated chocolate for garnish, optional

MAKES 12 CUPCAKES

Position a rack in the middle of the oven and preheat to 350°F. Line a standard 12-cup muffin pan with paper or foil liners.

In a bowl, whisk together the flour, cocoa powder, baking powder, and salt. Place the chocolate and butter in a large heatproof bowl set over (but not touching) simmering water in a saucepan; stir frequently until melted and smooth, about 5 minutes. Remove the bowl from the saucepan; let the mixture cool to room temperature, 10–15 minutes.

Using a wooden spoon, stir the sugar into the chocolate mixture until combined. Stir in the eggs one at a time, beating until combined after each addition, and then beat in the vanilla. Gently fold in the flour mixture just until no traces of flour remain; do not overmix.

Divide the batter evenly among the prepared muffin cups, filling each about three-fourths full. Bake until a toothpick inserted into the center of a cupcake comes out with only a few moist crumbs attached, 22–24 minutes. Let the cupcakes cool in the pan on a wire rack for 5 minutes. Transfer the cupcakes to the wire rack and let cool completely, about 1 hour.

Frost the cupcakes with the buttercream, garnish with grated chocolate, if using, and serve. (The frosted cupcakes can be refrigerated in an airtight container for up to 3 days; bring to room temperature before serving.)

Devil's Food Cupcakes

A rich chocolate glaze adds to the devilishly dark goodness of these cupcakes. Devil's Food Cupcakes are also great topped with any flavor of buttercream (page 105), Meringue Frosting (page 108), or Marshmallow Frosting (page 109).

1 cup all-purpose flour

¼ cup unsweetened cocoa powder

¾ tsp baking soda

¼ tsp salt

½ cup granulated sugar

½ cup firmly packed light brown sugar

4 tbsp unsalted butter, at room temperature

1 large egg, at room temperature

1 tsp vanilla extract

½ cup lukewarm water

¼ cup buttermilk

Rich Chocolate Glaze (page 112)

Sugared Flowers (page 118), optional

MAKES 12 CUPCAKES

Position a rack in the middle of the oven and preheat to 350°F. Line a standard 12-cup muffin pan with paper or foil liners.

Sift together the flour, cocoa powder, baking soda, and salt into a bowl. In another bowl, with an electric mixer on medium-high speed, beat the granulated sugar, brown sugar, and butter together until light and fluffy, 2–3 minutes. Add the egg and vanilla and beat until combined. Add the flour mixture in 3 additions, alternating with the water and buttermilk, beating on low speed until just combined; scrape down the sides of the bowl as needed. Beat on medium-high speed just until no traces of flour remain, about 30 seconds; do not overbeat.

Divide the batter evenly among the prepared muffin cups, filling each about three-fourths full. Bake until a toothpick inserted into the center of a cupcake comes out clean, 18–20 minutes. Let the cupcakes cool in the pan on a wire rack for 5 minutes. Transfer the cupcakes to the wire rack and let cool completely, about 1 hour.

Spoon the chocolate glaze over the cupcakes. (The glazed cupcakes can be refrigerated in an airtight container for up to 4 days; bring to room temperature before finishing and serving.) Garnish the cupcakes with the sugared flowers, if using, and serve.

Carrot Cake Cupcakes

These moist, lightly spiced cupcakes, topped with sweet and tangy cream cheese frosting, are delicious the day they are baked, but they're even better if they're made ahead and their flavors are given a chance to meld for 1–2 days.

1½ cups all-purpose flour

1 tsp baking powder

½ tsp baking soda

½ tsp salt

½ tsp ground cinnamon

1½ cups finely grated carrots (about 3 carrots)

1 cup sugar

¾ cup vegetable oil

2 large eggs, at room temperature

¼ cup buttermilk

½ tsp vanilla extract

Cream Cheese Frosting (page 106)

Candied Carrots (page 119), optional

MAKES 12 CUPCAKES

Position a rack in the middle of the oven and preheat to 350°F. Line a standard 12-cup muffin pan with paper or foil liners.

In a bowl, whisk together the flour, baking powder, baking soda, salt, and cinnamon. In another bowl, whisk together the grated carrots, sugar, oil, eggs, buttermilk, and vanilla to combine. Using a rubber spatula, fold the flour mixture into the carrot mixture until completely combined.

Divide the batter evenly among the prepared muffin cups, filling each about two-thirds full. Bake until golden brown and a toothpick inserted in the center of a cupcake comes out clean, 20–25 minutes. Let the cupcakes cool in the pan on a wire rack for 5 minutes. Transfer the cupcakes to the wire rack and let cool completely, about 1 hour.

Frost the cupcakes with the cream cheese frosting. (The frosted cupcakes can be refrigerated in an airtight container for up to 5 days; bring to room temperature before finishing and serving.) Garnish the cupcakes with the candied carrots, if using, and serve.

Gingerbread Cupcakes

Gingerbread cupcakes, heady with spices, get a boost of bracing flavor from grated fresh ginger. For a little extra kick, add a teaspoon of grated fresh ginger to the lemon glaze before spooning it onto the cupcakes.

1¼ cups all-purpose flour

1¼ tsp baking powder

1 tsp ground ginger

1 tsp ground cinnamon

¼ tsp ground allspice

Pinch freshly grated nutmeg

¼ tsp salt

½ cup firmly packed light brown sugar

⅓ cup light molasses

4 tbsp unsalted butter, at room temperature

1 large egg, at room temperature

2 tsp freshly grated ginger

⅓ cup whole milk

Lemon Glaze (page 114)

MAKES 12 CUPCAKES

Position a rack in the middle of the oven and preheat to 350°F. Line a standard 12-cup muffin pan with paper or foil liners.

In a bowl, whisk together the flour, baking powder, ground ginger, cinnamon, allspice, nutmeg, and salt. In another bowl, using an electric mixer on medium-high speed, beat the brown sugar, molasses, and butter together until light and fluffy, 2–3 minutes. Add the egg and fresh ginger and beat until combined. Add the flour mixture in 3 additions, alternating with the milk in 2 additions, beating on low speed until just combined; scrape down the sides of the bowl as needed.

Divide the batter evenly among the prepared muffin cups, filling each about three-fourths full. Bake until a toothpick inserted in the center of a cupcake comes out clean, about 20 minutes. Let the cupcakes cool in the pan on a wire rack for 5 minutes. Transfer the cupcakes to the wire rack and let cool completely, about 1 hour.

Spoon the glaze over the cupcakes and serve. (The glazed cupcakes can be refrigerated in an airtight container for up to 4 days; bring to room temperature before serving.)

Mocha Cupcakes

Coffee and chocolate combine perfectly in these mildly sweet cupcakes that appeal to adult taste buds. Coarsely chopped chocolate–covered espresso beans are a flavorful garnish for sprinkling onto the frosted cupcakes.

1⅓ cups all-purpose flour

⅓ cup unsweetened cocoa powder

1 tsp baking powder

½ tsp baking soda

¼ tsp salt

½ cup whole milk

½ cup strong brewed coffee, at room temperature

½ cup unsalted butter, at room temperature

½ cup granulated sugar

½ cup firmly packed light brown sugar

1 large egg, at room temperature

Coffee Buttercream (page 105)

MAKES 12 CUPCAKES

Position a rack in the middle of the oven and preheat to 350°F. Line a standard 12-cup muffin pan with paper or foil liners.

Sift together the flour, cocoa powder, baking powder, baking soda, and salt into a bowl. In a small bowl, combine the milk and brewed coffee. In a medium bowl, using an electric mixer on medium-high speed, beat the butter and sugars together until light and fluffy, 2–3 minutes. Add the egg and beat until combined. Add the flour mixture in 3 additions, alternating with the milk mixture in 2 additions, beating on low speed until just combined; scrape down the sides of the bowl as needed.

Divide the batter evenly among the prepared muffin cups, filling each about three-fourths full. Bake until a toothpick inserted in the center of a cupcake comes out clean, 22–24 minutes. Let the cupcakes cool in the pan on a wire rack for 5 minutes. Transfer the cupcakes to the wire rack and let cool completely, about 1 hour.

Frost the cupcakes with the buttercream and serve. (The frosted cupcakes can be refrigerated in an airtight container for up to 3 days; bring to room temperature before serving.)

Chai & Honey Cupcakes

Spiced chai tea and floral honey flavor these cupcakes. Chunks of golden honeycomb make beautiful and unusual garnishes. Look for honeycomb in natural food stores. If it's unavailable, simply drizzle the cupcakes with additional honey just before serving.

3 chai-spice tea bags

⅔ cup boiling water

1¼ cups all-purpose flour

¾ cup firmly packed light brown sugar

1 tsp baking soda

¼ tsp salt

¼ cup honey

4 tbsp unsalted butter, melted

¼ cup buttermilk

1 large egg, at room temperature

Honey Whipped Cream (page 110)

Honeycomb, cut into 1-inch pieces, for garnish, optional

MAKES 12 CUPCAKES

Position a rack in the middle of the oven and preheat to 350°F. Line a standard 12-cup muffin pan with paper or foil liners. In a small bowl, steep the tea bags in the boiling water for 5 minutes. Discard the tea bags and let the tea cool to room temperature.

In a bowl, whisk together the flour, brown sugar, baking soda, and salt. In a large bowl, combine the honey, melted butter, buttermilk, and egg. Add the flour mixture and, using an electric mixer on medium speed, beat until just combined, about 2 minutes. Add the cooled tea and beat until just combined, scraping down the sides of the bowl as needed.

Divide the batter evenly among the prepared muffin cups, filling each about three-fourths full. Bake until a toothpick inserted in the center of a cupcake comes out clean, 18–20 minutes. Let the cupcakes cool in the pan on a wire rack for 5 minutes. Transfer the cupcakes to the wire rack and let cool completely, about 1 hour. (The unfrosted cupcakes can be refrigerated in an airtight container for up to 3 days; bring to room temperature before frosting and garnishing.)

Frost the cupcakes with the honey cream, garnish with the honeycomb pieces, if using, and serve right away.

Crumbcake Cupcakes

These cupcakes are mostly buttery crumb topping baked on top of just a little bit of cake. They're the perfect treat for those who love the crumb topping on coffee cake more than the cake itself. Of course, a cup of joe is a perfect accompaniment.

FOR THE TOPPING

1¼ cups all-purpose flour

½ cup firmly packed light brown sugar

1½ tsp ground cinnamon

¼ tsp salt

¾ cup unsalted butter, at room temperature

1 cup all-purpose flour

½ tsp baking powder

½ tsp baking soda

¼ tsp salt

½ cup granulated sugar

4 tbsp unsalted butter, at room temperature

1 large egg, at room temperature

1 tsp vanilla extract

½ cup buttermilk

MAKES 12 CUPCAKES

Position a rack in the middle of the oven and preheat to 350°F. Lightly spray a standard 12-cup muffin pan with nonstick cooking spray.

To make the topping, in a bowl, combine the flour, brown sugar, cinnamon, and salt. Cut in the butter, using a pastry blender or 2 knives, until large, moist crumbs form. (The topping can be stored in an airtight container in the refrigerator for up to 4 days.)

In a bowl, whisk together the flour, baking powder, baking soda, and salt. In another bowl, using an electric mixer on medium-high speed, beat the granulated sugar and butter together until light and fluffy, 2–3 minutes. Add the egg and vanilla; beat until combined. Add the buttermilk in 3 additions, alternating with the flour mixture in 2 additions, beating on low speed until just combined; scrape down the sides of the bowl as needed.

Divide the batter evenly among the prepared muffin cups, filling each about one-half full. Top with the crumb topping, dividing it evenly. Bake until golden brown and a toothpick inserted into the center of a cupcake comes out clean, 18–20 minutes. Let the cupcakes cool in the pan on a wire rack for 5 minutes. Transfer the cupcakes to the wire rack and let cool completely, about 1 hour. Serve at room temperature. (The cupcakes can be stored at room temperature in an airtight container for up to 4 days.)

Strawberry Cupcakes

Fresh strawberries and strawberry jam mixed into the batter give these cupcakes a just-picked strawberry flavor, and a few drops of red food coloring adds a subtle pink hue. Select the prettiest strawberries from the batch to use as the garnish.

2 tbsp strawberry jam or preserves

¼ cup finely chopped fresh strawberries, plus 12 whole strawberries for garnish

1¼ cups all-purpose flour

1¼ tsp baking powder

¼ tsp salt

¾ cup sugar

½ cup unsalted butter, at room temperature

3 large egg whites, at room temperature

½ tsp vanilla extract

4 drops red food coloring

⅓ cup whole milk

Strawberry Buttercream (page 105)

MAKES 12 CUPCAKES

Position a rack in the middle of the oven and preheat to 350°F. Line a standard 12-cup muffin pan with paper or foil liners. In a small bowl, stir together the jam and chopped fresh strawberries.

In a bowl, whisk together the flour, baking powder, and salt. In another bowl, using an electric mixer on medium-high speed, beat the sugar and butter together until light and fluffy, 2–3 minutes. Add the egg whites, vanilla, and red food coloring and beat until combined. Add the flour mixture in 3 additions, alternating with the milk in 2 additions, beating on low speed until just combined; scrape down the sides of the bowl as needed. Fold in the strawberry mixture until just combined.

Divide the batter evenly among the prepared muffin cups, filling each about three-fourths full. Bake until lightly golden and a toothpick inserted in the center of a cupcake comes out clean, about 25 minutes. Let the cupcakes cool in the pan on a wire rack for 5 minutes. Transfer the cupcakes to the wire rack and let cool completely, about 1 hour.

Frost the cupcakes with the buttercream. (The frosted cupcakes can be refrigerated in an airtight container for up to 3 days; bring to room temperature before finishing.) Top each with a fresh strawberry and serve.

on Poppy Seed Cupcakes

These cupcakes sparkle with fresh lemon flavor. The lemon essence comes from a combination of grated lemon zest, lemon extract, and a sweet-tart lemon glaze; the poppy seeds add a gentle crunch. Serve the cupcakes with freshly brewed tea.

1 cup all-purpose flour

1½ tbsp poppy seeds

1 tsp baking powder

¼ teaspoon salt

¾ cup sugar

½ cup plus 2 tbsp unsalted butter, at room temperature

2 large eggs, at room temperature

1 tsp freshly grated lemon zest

½ tsp lemon extract

¼ cup sour cream

Lemon Glaze (page 114)

MAKES 12 CUPCAKES

Position a rack in the middle of the oven and preheat to 350°F. Lightly spray a standard 12-cup muffin pan with nonstick cooking spray.

In a bowl, whisk together the flour, poppy seeds, baking powder, and salt. In another bowl, using an electric mixer on medium-high speed, beat the sugar and butter together until light and fluffy, 2–3 minutes. Add the eggs, lemon zest, and lemon extract, and beat until combined. Add the flour mixture and beat on low speed until just combined, about 1 minute. Add the sour cream and beat until just combined; scrape down the sides of the bowl as needed.

Divide the batter evenly among the prepared muffin cups, filling each about three-fourths full. Bake until golden brown and a toothpick inserted in the center of a cupcake comes out clean, 18–20 minutes. Let the cupcakes cool in the pan on a wire rack for 5 minutes. Transfer the cupcakes to the wire rack and let cool completely, about 1 hour.

Spoon the glaze over the cupcakes and serve. (The glazed cupcakes can be refrigerated in an airtight container for up to 4 days; bring to room temperature before serving.)

Fruit & Nut Cupcakes

Triple Berry Cupcakes

Raspberry jam is baked into the center of vanilla cupcakes, adding a delightful burst of berry flavor. On top, cream cheese frosting is a nice counterpoint to the fresh berries. Make these cupcakes at the height of summer, when berries are at their best.

Batter for Vanilla Cupcakes (page 23)

¼ **cup raspberry jam or preserves**

Cream Cheese Frosting (page 106)

1½ **pints mixed berries, such as raspberries, blackberries, strawberries, and blueberries**

MAKES 12 CUPCAKES

Position a rack in the middle of the oven and preheat to 350°F. Line a standard 12-cup muffin pan with paper or foil liners.

Divide the cupcake batter evenly among the prepared muffin cups, filling each about three-fourths full. Drop 1 teaspoon raspberry jam onto the center of each (the jam will sink into the cupcakes as they bake). Bake until lightly golden a toothpick inserted into the center of a cupcake comes out with only a few cake crumbs and raspberry jam attached, 18–20 minutes. Let the cupcakes cool in the pan on a wire rack for 5 minutes. Transfer the cupcakes to the wire rack and let cool completely, about 1 hour.

Frost the cupcakes with the cream cheese frosting. (The frosted cupcakes can be refrigerated in an airtight container for up to 3 days; bring to room temperature before finishing.) Top with an assortment of berries, dividing them evenly, and serve right away.

Grapefruit
& Buttermilk Cupcakes

These are treats for those who love the tangy, slightly bitter edge of fresh grapefruit. If you're making these cupcakes and find yourself without buttermilk, substitute 1 cup of milk into which 1 tablespoon of lemon juice has been stirred.

1½ cups all-purpose flour

¾ tsp baking powder

½ tsp baking soda

¼ tsp salt

1 cup sugar

4 tbsp unsalted butter, at room temperature

1 large egg, at room temperature

½ tsp vanilla extract

1 cup buttermilk

Grapefruit Curd (page 115)

Vanilla Buttercream (page 105)

12 pieces Candied Grapefruit Peel (page 117)

MAKES 12 CUPCAKES

Position a rack in the middle of the oven and preheat to 350°F. Line a standard 12-cup muffin pan with paper or foil liners.

In a bowl, whisk together the flour, baking powder, baking soda, and salt. In another bowl, using an electric mixer on medium-high speed, beat the sugar and butter together until light and fluffy, 2–3 minutes. Add the egg and vanilla and beat until combined. Add the flour mixture in 3 additions, alternating with the buttermilk in 2 additions, beating on low speed until just combined; scrape down the sides of the bowl as needed.

Divide the batter evenly among the prepared muffin cups, filling each about three-fourths full. Bake until lightly golden and a toothpick inserted in the center of a cupcake comes out clean, 24–26 minutes. Let the cupcakes cool in the pan on a wire rack for 5 minutes. Transfer the cupcakes to the wire rack and let cool completely, about 1 hour.

Using a paring knife, hollow out a 1½-inch round piece about 1 inch deep from the center of each cupcake (see page 14). Fill each hollow with a generous tablespoon of grapefruit curd, letting the curd spread out onto the cupcake's surface. Frost the filled cupcakes with the buttercream. (The filled and frosted cupcakes can be refrigerated in an airtight container for up to 3 days; bring to room temperature before finishing.) Top each cupcake with a piece of candied grapefruit peel and serve.

Rose Water & Raspberry Cupcakes ....

Pretty in pink, these cupcakes are perfect for baby or bridal showers or afternoon tea parties. Rose water flavors both the cupcakes and the glaze with a sweet, delicate floral essence. Look for rose water in specialty food stores and Middle Eastern markets.

1¼ cups all-purpose flour

1 tsp baking powder

¼ tsp salt

¾ cup confectioners' sugar

½ cup unsalted butter, at room temperature

1 tbsp rose water

2 large eggs, at room temperature

½ cup whole milk

Rose Water Glaze (page 114)

1 pint raspberries

Sugared petals (page 118), using pale pink rose petals

MAKES 12 CUPCAKES

Position a rack in the middle of the oven and preheat to 350°F. Line a standard 12-cup muffin pan with paper or foil liners.

In a small bowl, whisk together the flour, baking powder, and salt. In another bowl, with an electric mixer on medium-high speed, beat the confectioners' sugar and butter together until light and fluffy, 2–3 minutes. Add the rose water and the eggs, one at a time, beating on low speed until combined after each addition. Add the flour mixture in 3 additions, alternating with the milk in 2 additions, beating on low speed until just combined; scrape down the sides of the bowl as needed.

Divide the batter evenly among the prepared muffin cups, filling each about three-fourths full. Bake until lightly golden and a toothpick inserted into the center of a cupcake comes out clean, 15–18 minutes. Let the cupcakes cool in the pan on a wire rack for 5 minutes. Transfer the cupcakes to the wire rack and let cool completely, about 1 hour.

Spoon the glaze over the cupcakes. (The glazed cupcakes can be refrigerated in an airtight container for up to 3 days; bring to room temperature before finishing.) Top each cupcake with the fresh raspberries and the sugared rose petals, dividing evenly, and serve.

Lemon Blueberry Crunch Cupcakes

The crunch in these cupcakes comes from a generous sprinkling of sugar on top of the fresh blueberries just before baking. A drizzle of lemon glaze adds a finished looked as well as a tangy lemon flavor. Serve these cupcakes for brunch or for dessert.

1¼ cups all-purpose flour

½ tsp baking powder

½ tsp baking soda

¼ tsp salt

¾ cup sugar, plus 2 tbsp for topping

4 tbsp unsalted butter, at room temperature

1 large egg, at room temperature

1 tsp lemon extract

1 tsp finely grated lemon zest

¾ cup sour cream

1¼ cups fresh blueberries

Lemon Glaze (page 114)

MAKES 12 CUPCAKES

Position a rack in the middle of the oven and preheat to 350°F. Line a standard 12-cup muffin pan with paper or foil liners.

In a small bowl, whisk together the flour, baking powder, baking soda, and salt. In a large bowl, with an electric mixer on medium-high speed, beat the ¾ cup of the sugar and the butter together until light and fluffy, 2–3 minutes. Add the egg, lemon extract, and zest and beat on medium speed until combined. With the mixer on low speed, add the flour mixture and the sour cream, beating until just combined; scrape down the sides of the bowl as needed.

Divide the batter evenly among the prepared muffin cups, filling each about three-fourths full. Arrange the blueberries in a single layer on top of the batter, dividing evenly, then sprinkle with the remaining 2 tablespoons sugar, dividing evenly. Bake until the blueberries burst, the centers of the cupcakes are lightly golden, and a toothpick inserted in the center of a cupcake comes out clean, 18–20 minutes. Let the cupcakes cool completely in the pan on a wire rack, about 1 hour. Remove the cupcakes from the pan. (The cooled cupcakes can be refrigerated in an airtight container for up to 3 days; bring to room temperature before finishing.) Drizzle the glaze over the cupcakes and serve right away.

Sour Cherry–Almond Cupcakes

Sour cherries and almonds are a classic flavor pairing. The season for sour cherries is early summer, but don't blink or you'll miss it. If you can't find fresh sour cherries, look for frozen; before use, thaw frozen sour cherries in a colander to drain off excess juice.

1 cup all-purpose flour

1 tsp baking powder

¼ tsp salt

¾ cup plus 2 tbsp sugar

¼ cup almond paste

6 tbsp unsalted butter, at room temperature

3 large eggs, separated, at room temperature

½ tsp vanilla extract

½ cup whole milk

1 cup pitted sour cherries, roughly chopped

Vanilla Glaze (page 114)

MAKES 12 CUPCAKES

Position a rack in the middle of the oven and preheat to 350°F. Line a standard 12-cup muffin pan with paper or foil liners. In a bowl, whisk together the flour, baking powder, and salt. In another bowl, using an electric mixer on medium speed, beat the ¾ cup sugar with the almond paste until the mixture resembles coarse meal. Add the butter and beat on high speed until light and fluffy, 2–3 minutes. Add the egg yolks and vanilla and beat until combined. Add the flour mixture in 3 additions, alternating with the milk in 2 additions, beating on low speed until just combined; scrape down the sides of the bowl as needed.

In a large clean bowl, using an electric mixer with clean attachments on medium-high speed, beat the egg whites until foamy. Slowly add the remaining 2 tablespoons sugar and beat continuously until soft peaks form. Gently fold a third of the egg white mixture into the batter to lighten. Fold in the remaining whites and the sour cherries until no white streaks remain.

Divide the batter evenly among the prepared muffin cups, filling each about one-half full. Bake until a toothpick inserted in the center of a cupcake comes out clean, 18–20 minutes. Let the cupcakes cool in the pan on a wire rack for 5 minutes. Transfer the cupcakes to the wire rack and let cool completely, about 1 hour. Spoon the glaze over the cupcakes and serve. (The glazed cupcakes can be refrigerated in an airtight container for up to 4 days; bring to room temperature before serving.)

Lime Meringue Cupcakes

Lemon meringue pie inspired these cupcakes that combine rich, buttery cake, thick, puckery lime curd, and light, sweet meringue frosting. Tall, curvy peaks of meringue, lightly browned with a kitchen torch, make for a dramatic presentation.

Batter for Vanilla Cupcakes (page 23)

Lime Curd (page 115)

Meringue Frosting (page 108)

MAKES 12 CUPCAKES

Position a rack in the middle of the oven and preheat to 350°F. Lightly spray a standard 12-cup standard muffin pan with nonstick cooking spray.

Divide the cupcake batter evenly among the prepared muffin cups, filling each about three-fourths full. Bake until lightly golden and a toothpick inserted into the center of a cupcake comes out clean, 18–20 minutes. Let the cupcakes cool in the pan on a wire rack for 5 minutes. Transfer the cupcakes to the wire rack and let cool completely, about 1 hour.

Using a paring knife, halve each cupcake horizontally (see page 14). Spread about 2 teaspoons lime curd on each cupcake bottom, then replace the tops. Spread each cupcake top with about 2 teaspoons lime curd, then frost with the meringue frosting. Using a kitchen torch, lightly brown the meringue. (The finished cupcakes can be refrigerated in an airtight container for up to 2 days; bring to room temperature before serving.)

Tangerine Cupcakes

The texture of these cupcakes is fine and dense, very much like pound cake. The batter can also be baked as eight 3½- by 2½-inch miniature loaves (spray the pans with nonstick cooking spray before filling). They will take about 25 minutes to bake.

1¼ cups all-purpose flour

1¼ tsp baking powder

¼ tsp salt

¼ cup sour cream

2 tbsp vegetable oil

1 tbsp fresh tangerine juice

1½ tsp finely grated tangerine zest

¼ tsp orange extract

¾ cup sugar

6 tbsp unsalted butter, at room temperature

2 large eggs, at room temperature

Tangerine Glaze (page 114)

MAKES 12 CUPCAKES

Position a rack in the middle of the oven and preheat to 350°F. Line a standard 12-cup muffin pan with paper or foil liners.

In a bowl, whisk together the flour, baking powder, and salt. In a small bowl, stir together the sour cream, oil, tangerine juice and zest, and orange extract. In another bowl, with an electric mixer on medium-high speed, beat the sugar and butter together until light and fluffy, 2–3 minutes. Add the eggs, one at a time, beating well after each addition. Add the flour mixture in 3 additions, alternating with the sour cream mixture in 2 additions, beating on low speed until just combined; scrape down the sides of the bowl as needed.

Divide the batter evenly among the prepared muffin cups, filling each about three-fourths full. Bake until lightly golden and a toothpick inserted in the center of a cupcake comes out clean, 18–20 minutes. Let the cupcakes cool completely in the pan on a wire rack, about 1 hour. Remove the cupcakes from the pan and set aside until ready to serve.

Spoon the glaze over each cupcake and serve. (The glazed cupcakes can be refrigerated in an airtight container for up to 4 days; bring to room temperature before serving.)

Apple Spice Cupcakes

Large chunks of apple keep these cupcakes exceptionally moist and give them a rustic, hearty texture. Use either tart or sweet apples, such as Granny Smith or Fuji. Just make sure that they have a crisp, firm texture.

½ cup unsalted butter, at room temperature

3 apples (about 1 lb), peeled, cored, and cut into 1-inch chunks

2 tbsp plus ¾ cup sugar

1 cup all-purpose flour

¾ tsp baking powder

½ tsp salt

¼ tsp baking soda

½ tsp ground cinnamon

¼ tsp ground allspice

Pinch freshly grated nutmeg

2 large eggs, at room temperature

½ tsp vanilla extract

¼ cup sour cream

Honey–Cream Cheese Frosting (page 106)

MAKES 12 CUPCAKES

Position a rack in the middle of the oven and preheat to 350°F. Line a standard 12-cup muffin pan with paper or foil liners. In a saucepan over medium-high heat, melt 2 tablespoons of the butter. Add the apple chunks and the 2 tablespoons of sugar and cook, stirring often, until the apples are translucent and soft, 5–7 minutes; set aside to cool.

In a bowl, whisk together the flour, baking powder, salt, baking soda, cinnamon, allspice, and nutmeg. In another bowl, with an electric mixer on medium-high speed, beat the remaining 6 tablespoons butter and the ¾ cup sugar together until light and fluffy, 2–3 minutes. Add the eggs and vanilla and beat until combined. Slowly add the flour mixture and beat on low speed until combined. Add the sour cream and reserved apple mixture, beating until just combined; scrape down the sides of the bowl as needed.

Divide the batter evenly among the prepared muffin cups, filling each about two-thirds full. Bake until golden brown and a toothpick inserted into the center of a cupcake comes out clean, 18–20 minutes. Let the cupcakes cool in the pan on a wire rack for 5 minutes. Transfer the cupcakes to the wire rack and let cool completely, about 1 hour.

Frost the cupcakes with the frosting and serve. (The frosted cupcakes can be refrigerated in an airtight container for up to 4 days; bring to room temperature before serving.)

Coconut-Lime Cupcakes

Classic coconut cake is filled with a bracing lime curd to create these breezy, tropical-flavored treats. Chopping the coconut that goes into the cupcake batter ensures a tender, delicately textured cake and lots of coconut flavor in every bite.

⅓ cup sweetened shredded coconut, plus 1 cup for garnish

1 cup all-purpose flour

1¼ tsp baking powder

¼ tsp salt

¾ cup plus 2 tbsp sugar

½ cup unsalted butter, at room temperature

1 large egg plus 1 large egg white, at room temperature

1 tsp vanilla extract

½ cup coconut milk

¾ cup Lime Curd (page 115)

Coconut Buttercream (page 105)

MAKES 12 CUPCAKES

Position a rack in the middle of the oven and preheat to 350°F. Line a standard 12-cup muffin pan with paper or foil liners.

Coarsely chop the ⅓ cup of shredded coconut. In a bowl, whisk together the flour, baking powder, salt, and the chopped coconut. In another bowl, with an electric mixer on medium-high speed, beat the sugar and butter together until light and fluffy, 2–3 minutes. Add the egg, egg white, and vanilla and beat until combined. Add the flour mixture in 3 additions, alternating with the coconut milk in 2 additions, beating on low speed until just combined; scrape down the sides of the bowl as needed.

Divide the batter evenly among the prepared muffin cups, filling each about three-fourths full. Bake until lightly golden and a toothpick inserted in the center of a cupcake comes out clean, 18–20 minutes. Let the cupcakes cool completely in the pan on a wire rack for 5 minutes. Transfer the cupcakes to the wire rack and let cool completely, about 1 hour.

Using a paring knife, hollow out a 1½-inch round piece about 1 inch deep from the center of each cupcake (see page 14). Fill each hollow with about 1 tablespoon lime curd. Frost the filled cupcakes with the buttercream and sprinkle with the remaining 1 cup coconut, dividing it evenly. (The filled and frosted cupcakes can be refrigerated in an airtight container for up to 4 days; bring to room temperature before serving.)

Mini Strawberry Cheesecakes

These little indulgences are scaled-down versions of a dessert favorite: the classic New York cheesecake. They combine the sweet fruitiness of fresh strawberries with the rich creaminess of cheesecake, and they taste every bit as luscious as any full-sized version.

FOR THE TOPPING

1 lb fresh strawberries, hulled and cut in half

½ cup plus 2 tbsp sugar

1 tbsp fresh lemon juice

FOR THE FILLING

1¼ lb cream cheese, at room temperature

¾ cup sugar

½ tsp vanilla extract

¼ cup sour cream

2 large eggs, at room temperature

3 tbsp all-purpose flour

MAKES 24 MINI CUPCAKES

To make the topping, in a nonreactive saucepan, combine ½ pound of the strawberries with the sugar. Use a fork to gently mash the strawberries. Cook over medium-high heat until the strawberries are softened, about 3 minutes. Remove from the heat and stir in the remaining ½ pound strawberries and lemon juice. Transfer to a small bowl and let cool completely. (The topping can be refrigerated in an airtight container for up to 2 days.)

Position a rack in the middle of the oven and preheat to 350°F. Line a 24-cup miniature muffin pan with miniature paper or foil liners. To make the filling, in a bowl, using an electric mixer on medium-high speed, beat the cream cheese until fluffy, about 3 minutes. With the mixer on low speed, gradually add the sugar and beat until smooth; scrape down the sides of the bowl as needed. Add the vanilla and sour cream and beat until combined. Add the eggs, one at a time, beating well after each; add the flour and beat until combined.

Divide the cream cheese filling evenly among the prepared muffin cups, filling each about ¾ full. Bake until the cheesecakes are just set in the center, about 15 minutes. Let the cheesecakes cool in the pan on a wire rack for 5 minutes. Using a small offset spatula, transfer the cheesecakes to the wire rack and let cool completely, about 45 minutes.

Refrigerate the cheesecakes in an airtight container at least overnight or for up to 3 days. Spoon about 1 tablespoon of the strawberry topping onto each chilled cheesecake and serve right away.

Rum Raisin Cupcakes

To make a garnish for these cupcakes, simmer 1 cup of dark rum with 2 tablespoons of sugar over medium-high heat until syrupy. Stir in 2 tablespoons each dark and golden raisins and let cool to room temperature. Divide among the frosted cupcakes.

⅓ cup dark rum

¼ cup dark raisins

¼ cup golden raisins

1¼ cups all-purpose flour

1 tsp baking powder

1 tsp ground cinnamon

¼ tsp ground allspice

¼ tsp salt

1 cup sugar

6 tbsp unsalted butter, at room temperature

1 large egg, at room temperature

1 tsp vanilla extract

½ cup whole milk

¾ cup walnuts, toasted (see page 8) and coarsely chopped

Rum Buttercream (page 105)

MAKES 12 CUPCAKES

In a bowl, combine the rum and raisins; let stand for at least 30 minutes or for up to 1 hour. Position a rack in the middle of the oven and preheat to 350°F. Line a standard 12-cup muffin pan with paper or foil liners.

In a bowl, whisk together the flour, baking powder, cinnamon, allspice, and salt. In another bowl, with an electric mixer on medium-high speed, beat the sugar and butter together until light and fluffy, 2–3 minutes. Add the egg and vanilla and beat on medium speed until combined. Add the flour mixture in 3 additions, alternating with the milk in 2 additions, beating on low speed until just combined; scrape down the sides of the bowl as needed. Add the rum-soaked raisin mixture and the chopped toasted walnuts; beat on low speed until just combined.

Divide the batter evenly among the prepared muffin cups, filling each about three-fourths full. Bake until lightly golden and a toothpick inserted in the center of a cupcake comes out clean, 18–20 minutes. Let the cupcakes cool completely in the pan on a wire rack, about 1 hour. Remove the cupcakes from the pan and set aside until ready to serve.

Frost the cupcakes with the buttercream and serve. (The frosted cupcakes can be refrigerated in an airtight container for up to 3 days; bring to room temperature before serving.)

Banana Caramel Cupcakes

Tropical bananas and toasty caramel have an undeniable flavor affinity that's the starring attraction of these cupcakes. When mixing the batter, be sure to fold gently after adding the banana mixture—overmixing could make the cupcakes tough.

1¼ cups cake flour

¾ tsp baking soda

¾ tsp baking powder

¼ tsp salt

1 large, ripe banana (about 8 oz)

2 tbsp sour cream

¾ cup firmly packed light brown sugar

½ cup unsalted butter, at room temperature

1 large egg, at room temperature

½ tsp vanilla extract

½ tsp finely grated lemon zest

Banana Buttercream (page 105)

Caramel Drizzle (page 116)

MAKES 12 CUPCAKES

Position a rack in the middle of the oven and preheat to 350°F. Line a standard 12-cup muffin pan with paper or foil liners.

Sift together the flour, baking soda, baking powder, and salt into a bowl. In a small bowl, use a fork to mash together the banana and sour cream. In a large bowl, using an electric mixer on medium-high speed, beat the brown sugar and butter together until light and fluffy, 2–3 minutes. Add the egg, vanilla, and lemon zest and beat until combined, scraping down the sides of the bowl as needed. Add flour mixture and beat on low speed until just combined; scrape down the sides of the bowl as needed. Fold in the banana mixture until just combined; do not overmix.

Divide the batter evenly among the prepared muffin cups, filling each about one-half full. Bake until lightly golden and a toothpick inserted into the center of a cupcake comes out clean, 18–20 minutes. Let the cupcakes cool in the pan on a wire rack for 5 minutes. Transfer the cupcakes to the wire rack and let cool completely, about 1 hour.

Frost the cupcakes with the buttercream. (The frosted cupcakes can be refrigerated in an airtight container for up to 3 days; bring to room temperature before finishing.) Spoon the caramel drizzle over the top of each frosted cupcake and serve.

PB & J Cupcakes

These cupcakes are a riff on the old childhood standby, the peanut butter and jelly sandwich. Truthfully, adults love the flavor combination as much as kids do. Use your favorite type of jam to fill the cupcakes, and serve them with ice-cold milk.

**Batter for Vanilla Cupcakes
(page 23)**

**Peanut Butter Frosting
(page 107)**

¾ **cup fruit jam or preserves**

MAKES 12 CUPCAKES

Position a rack in the middle of the oven and preheat to 350°F. Lightly spray a standard 12-cup muffin pan with nonstick cooking spray.

Divide the batter evenly among the prepared muffin cups, filling each about three-fourths full. Bake until lightly golden and a toothpick inserted into the center of a cupcake comes out clean, 18–20 minutes. Let the cupcakes cool in the pan on the wire rack for 5 minutes. Transfer the cupcakes to the wire rack and let cool completely, about 1 hour.

Using a paring knife, halve each cupcake horizontally (see page 14). Spread about 1 tablespoon of jam on each cupcake bottom, then replace the tops. Frost with the buttercream and serve. (The filled and frosted cupcakes can be refrigerated in an airtight container for up to 1 day; bring to room temperature before serving.)

Pumpkin Pecan Cupcakes

Canned pumpkin works perfectly in this recipe, but if you're substituting cooked fresh pumpkin purée, drain off the excess moisture before use: Place the purée in a cheesecloth-lined strainer set over a large bowl and refrigerate it overnight.

1 cup all-purpose flour

1 tsp baking powder

½ tsp baking soda

¼ tsp salt

1 tsp ground cinnamon

½ tsp ground ginger

¼ tsp ground allspice

Pinch freshly grated nutmeg

1 cup canned pumpkin purée

1 cup sugar

½ cup vegetable oil

2 large eggs, at room temperature

1 cup pecans, toasted (see page 8) and coarsely chopped

Maple Glaze (page 114)

MAKES 12 CUPCAKES

Position a rack in the middle of the oven and preheat to 350°F. Line a standard 12-cup muffin pan with paper or foil liners.

In a bowl, whisk together the flour, baking powder, baking soda, salt, cinnamon, ginger, allspice, and nutmeg. In another bowl, whisk together the pumpkin purée, sugar, oil, and eggs. Add the flour mixture and whisk to combine completely. Stir in the chopped pecans.

Divide the batter evenly among the prepared muffin cups, filling each about three-fourths full. Bake until a toothpick inserted into the center of a cupcake comes out clean, 22–24 minutes. Let the cupcakes cool in the pan on a wire rack for 5 minutes. Transfer the cupcakes to the wire rack and let cool completely, about 1 hour.

Spoon the glaze over the cupcakes and serve. (The glazed cupcakes can be refrigerated in an airtight container for up to 4 days; bring to room temperature before serving.)

Hazelnut–Brown Butter Cupcakes

These simple yet elegant cupcakes have a rich, nutty, and buttery flavor. They're delicious served warm out of the oven with only dusting of confectioners' sugar, but they're simply irresistible served with vanilla ice cream.

½ cup hazelnuts

½ cup plus 2 tbsp unsalted butter, cut into 10 pieces

1 cup plus 2 tbsp confectioners' sugar, plus extra for dusting

1 cup all-purpose flour

¾ tsp baking powder

½ tsp baking soda

¼ tsp salt

4 large egg whites, at room temperature

MAKES 12 CUPCAKES

Position a rack in the middle of the oven and preheat to 350°F. Lightly spray a standard 12-cup standard muffin pan with nonstick cooking spray. Follow the instructions on page 8 to toast the hazelnuts, then transfer the nuts to a clean kitchen towel and rub together to remove the skins. Let cool completely.

In a saucepan, heat the butter over medium-low heat, whisking frequently, until fragrant and nutty brown, 5–6 minutes; set aside to cool slightly. Place the hazelnuts and ¼ cup of the confectioners' sugar in a food processor and pulse until finely chopped, about 1 minute. In a bowl, whisk together the flour, baking powder, baking soda, salt, the remaining ¾ cup plus 2 tablespoons confectioners' sugar, and the nut mixture. Add the egg whites and brown butter. Using an electric mixer on medium speed, mix until combined, about 2 minutes; scrape down the sides of the bowl as needed.

Divide the batter evenly among the prepared muffin cups, filling each about one-half full. Bake until lightly golden and a toothpick inserted in the center of a cupcake comes out clean, 18–22 minutes. Let the cupcakes cool in the pan on a wire rack for 5 minutes. Transfer the cupcakes to the wire rack, dust lightly with confectioners' sugar, and serve warm. (The cupcakes can be cooled completely and stored in an airtight container at room temperature for up to 2 days; reheat in a 300°F oven for 7–10 minutes, dust lightly with confectioners' sugar, and serve warm.)

Chocolate Cupcakes

Black Forest Cupcakes

These cupcakes are individually sized and deliciously eye-catching versions of the classic Black Forest Cake. Kirsch, a cherry-flavored brandy, gives the lightly sweetened whipped cream that stands in for frosting an extra measure of cherry flavor.

Devil's Food Cupcakes (page 28)

1½ cups fresh Bing cherries, pitted and cut in half, plus 12 whole unpitted cherries with stems for garnish

2 tbsp granulated sugar

1 tbsp kirsch

1 cup cold heavy cream

1 tbsp confectioners' sugar

MAKES 12 CUPCAKES

Bake and cool the cupcakes according to the recipe, then top with the Rich Chocolate Glaze. Set aside.

In a small saucepan over medium heat, combine the halved cherries, granulated sugar, and kirsch. Cook, stirring occasionally, until the cherries soften and the juice becomes syrupy, 5–7 minutes. Transfer to a small bowl, cover, and refrigerate until cold, at least 1 hour or for up to 1 day.

In a bowl, combine the cream and confectioners' sugar. Using an electric mixer on low speed, beat until slightly thickened, 1–2 minutes. Gradually increase the speed to medium-high and beat until the cream holds soft peaks, 2–3 minutes. Using a rubber spatula, gently fold the cherry mixture into the whipped cream, leaving streaks of red. Top the glazed cupcakes with the cherry–whipped cream mixture, garnish each with a whole cherry, and serve. (The finished cupcakes can be refrigerated in an airtight container for up to 1 day; let stand at room temperature for 10 minutes before serving.)

Mexican Chocolate Cupcakes

Sweet and cinnamon-scented Mexican chocolate is available in Latin markets and can often be found in the ethnic-foods aisle of grocery stores. If you can't find it, substitute semisweet chocolate and increase the ground cinnamon in the batter to 1 teaspoon.

1 cup all-purpose flour

¾ cup sugar

¼ cup unsweetened cocoa powder

¾ tsp baking soda

1 tsp ground cinnamon

¼ tsp salt

¾ cup lukewarm water

⅓ cup vegetable oil

¾ tsp white vinegar

½ cup finely grated Mexican chocolate (1 tablet), plus extra for garnish

Basic Buttercream (page 104)

MAKES 12 CUPCAKES

Position a rack in the middle of the oven and preheat to 350°F. Line a standard 12-cup muffin pan with paper or foil liners.

Sift together the flour, sugar, cocoa powder, baking soda, ½ teaspoon of the cinnamon, and the salt into a bowl. Add the water, oil, and vinegar to the flour mixture; using an electric mixer on medium speed, beat until combined. Add the ½ cup grated Mexican chocolate and beat on low speed until just incorporated; scrape down the sides of the bowl as needed.

Divide the batter evenly among the prepared muffin cups, filling each about three-fourths full. Bake until a toothpick inserted in the center of a cupcake comes out clean, 24–28 minutes. Let the cupcakes cool in the pan on a wire rack for 5 minutes. Transfer the cupcakes to the wire rack and let cool completely, about 1 hour.

Whisk the remaining ½ teaspoon of the cinnamon into the Basic Buttercream until combined. Frost the cupcakes with the buttercream, sprinkle with additional grated Mexican chocolate, and serve. (The finished cupcakes can be refrigerated in an airtight container for up to 4 days; bring to room temperature before serving.)

Red Velvet Cupcakes

The origins of red velvet cake are a little hazy, but it's widely recognized as a Southern creation. This cupcake version of the extra-mild chocolate cake is topped with a cream cheese frosting that's laced with buttered pecans, a decidedly Southern ingredient.

1¼ cups cake flour

2 tbsp unsweetened cocoa powder

¾ tsp baking powder

¼ tsp salt

½ cup buttermilk

1 tsp vanilla extract

½ tsp white vinegar

4 drops red food coloring

¾ cup sugar

4 tbsp unsalted butter, at room temperature

1 large egg, at room temperature

Cream Cheese Frosting with Buttered Pecans (page 106)

MAKES 12 CUPCAKES

Position a rack in the middle of the oven and preheat to 350°F. Line a standard 12-cup muffin pan with paper or foil liners.

Sift together the cake flour, cocoa powder, baking powder, and salt into a bowl. In a small bowl, whisk together the buttermilk, vanilla, vinegar, and red food coloring. In another bowl, using an electric mixer on medium-high speed, beat the sugar and butter together until light and fluffy, 2–3 minutes. Add the egg and beat until combined. Add the flour mixture in 3 additions, alternating with the buttermilk mixture in 2 additions, beating on low speed until combined; scrape down the sides of the bowl as needed.

Divide the batter evenly among the prepared muffin cups, filling each about three-fourths full. Bake until a toothpick inserted into the center of a cupcake comes out clean, 20–22 minutes. Let the cupcakes cool in the pan on a wire rack for 5 minutes. Transfer the cupcakes to the wire rack and let cool completely, about 1 hour.

Frost the cupcakes with the cream cheese–pecan frosting and serve. (The frosted cupcakes can be refrigerated in an airtight container for up to 4 days; bring to room temperature before serving.)

German Chocolate Cupcakes

If time permits, make these goodies in advance because their flavor and texture improve as they stand. To melt the chocolate, warm it in a heatproof bowl set over (but not touching) simmering water in a saucepan, stirring until melted and smooth.

1¼ cups all-purpose flour

¾ tsp baking soda

¼ tsp salt

¾ cup sugar

½ cup unsalted butter, at room temperature

1 large egg, at room temperature

½ tsp vanilla extract

2 oz semisweet chocolate, chopped, melted, and cooled to room temperature

¼ cup sour cream

½ cup whole milk

German Chocolate Topping (page 111)

MAKES 12 CUPCAKES

Position a rack in the middle of the oven and preheat to 350°F. Lightly spray a standard 12-cup muffin pan with nonstick cooking spray.

In a bowl, whisk together the flour, baking soda, and salt. In another bowl, using an electric mixer on medium-high speed, beat the sugar and butter together until light and fluffy, 2–3 minutes. Add the egg and vanilla and beat until combined. Add the melted chocolate and sour cream and beat on low speed until combined. Add the flour mixture in 3 additions, alternating with the milk in 2 additions, beating on low speed until just combined; scrape down the sides of the bowl as needed.

Divide the batter evenly among the prepared muffin cups, filling each about three-fourths full. Bake until a toothpick inserted in the center of a cupcake comes out clean, 18–20 minutes. Let the cupcakes cool in the pan on a wire rack for 5 minutes. Transfer the cupcakes to the wire rack and let cool completely, about 1 hour.

Using a paring knife, halve each cupcake horizontally (see page 14). Spread about 1 tablespoon of the topping on each cupcake bottom, then replace the tops. Top each cupcake with about 2 tablespoons topping and serve. (The finished cupcakes can be refrigerated in an airtight container for up to 4 days; bring to room temperature before serving.)

Mini Chocolate-Mint Cupcakes

These mini cupcakes have a moist, fudgy, brownie-like texture. They're flavored with cool peppermint and are topped with a minty chocolate buttercream. To make the batter, a good old-fashioned whisk works better than a mixer, and is easier to boot.

4 oz bittersweet chocolate, chopped

4 tbsp unsalted butter, cut into 4 pieces

¾ cup sugar

2 large eggs, at room temperature

½ tsp vanilla extract

¼ tsp peppermint extract

¼ tsp salt

¼ cup plus 2 tbsp all-purpose flour

Chocolate-Mint Buttercream (page 105)

MAKES 24 MINI CUPCAKES

Position a rack in the middle of the oven and preheat to 350°F. Line a 24-cup miniature muffin pan with miniature paper or foil liners. Place the chocolate and butter in a heatproof bowl set over (but not touching) simmering water in a saucepan; stir frequently until melted and smooth. Remove the bowl from the saucepan; let the mixture cool until it is room temperature.

Using a wooden spoon, stir the sugar into the melted chocolate mixture. Whisk in the eggs, one at a time, whisking until combined after each addition. Whisk in the vanilla and peppermint extracts and then the salt. Gently fold in the flour; do not overmix.

Divide the batter evenly among the prepared muffin cups, filling each about three-fourths full. Bake until the tops are crackly and a toothpick inserted in the center of a cupcake comes out with only a few moist crumbs attached, 18–20 minutes. Let the cupcakes cool completely in the pan on a wire rack, about 45 minutes. Remove the cupcakes from the pan.

Frost the cupcakes with buttercream and serve. (The frosted cupcakes can be refrigerated in an airtight container for up to 4 days; bring to room temperature before serving.)

Molten Chocolate Cupcakes

These cupcakes bake up as light as air and, as a surprise, have melted dark–chocolate centers hidden within. Cold, creamy vanilla ice cream or lightly sweetened whipped cream are perfect foils to these warm, chocolaty cupcakes.

3½ oz semisweet chocolate, chopped

4 tbsp unsalted butter, cut into 4 pieces

3 large eggs, separated, at room temperature

2 tbsp all-purpose flour

Pinch salt

¼ cup sugar

1 bittersweet chocolate bar (about 4 oz), broken evenly into 12 pieces

MAKES 12 CUPCAKES

Position a rack in the middle of the oven and preheat to 375°F. Lightly spray a standard 12-cup muffin pan with nonstick cooking spray. Place the semisweet chocolate and butter in a heatproof bowl set over (but not touching) simmering water in a saucepan; stir frequently until melted and smooth. Remove the bowl from the saucepan; let the mixture cool slightly.

Whisk the egg yolks into the chocolate mixture until well combined, about 30 seconds. Add the flour and whisk until combined.

In a clean bowl, using an electric mixer with clean attachments on medium-high speed, beat the egg whites and salt until foamy. Slowly add the sugar and beat continuously until soft peaks form. Using a whisk, gently fold a third of the egg whites into the chocolate mixture to lighten. Fold in the egg white mixture in 2 more additions until no white streaks remain.

Divide the batter among the prepared muffin cups, filling each about two-thirds full. Bake the cupcakes for 5 minutes and then remove the pan from the oven; working quickly, insert one piece of bittersweet chocolate into the center of each cupcake. Return the pan to the oven and bake until the cupcakes are well-risen and brown around the edges, 3–5 minutes more. Let the cupcakes cool briefly in the pan on a wire rack, about 5 minutes. Use a small offset spatula to transfer cupcakes to plates and serve right away.

Triple Chocolate Cupcakes

With milk chocolate cake, dark chocolate filling, and white chocolate frosting, these cupcakes are a chocolate lover's dream. To warm the Rich Chocolate Glaze to fill the cupcakes, heat it gently in a bowl set over, but not touching, simmering water.

3 oz milk chocolate, chopped

½ cup plus 3 tbsp unsalted butter, cut into 11 pieces

⅔ cup all-purpose flour

2½ tbsp unsweetened cocoa powder

¾ tsp baking powder

¼ tsp salt

¾ cup sugar

1 tsp vanilla extract

3 large eggs, at room temperature

¾ cup Rich Chocolate Glaze (page 112), warm

White Chocolate Buttercream (page 105)

MAKES 12 CUPCAKES

Position a rack in the middle of the oven and preheat to 350°F. Line a standard 12-cup muffin pan with paper or foil liners. Place the milk chocolate and butter in a large heatproof bowl set over (but not touching) simmering water in a saucepan; stir frequently until melted and smooth. Remove the bowl from the saucepan; let the mixture cool until it is room temperature.

In a bowl, whisk together the flour, cocoa powder, baking powder, and salt. Using a wooden spoon, stir the sugar into the chocolate mixture until combined. Stir in the vanilla and eggs, one at a time, stirring vigorously until smooth after each addition. Gently fold in the flour mixture; do not overmix.

Divide the batter evenly among the prepared muffin cups, filling each about three-fourths full. Bake until a toothpick inserted into the center of a cupcake comes out with only a few moist crumbs attached, 22–24 minutes. Let the cupcakes cool in the pan on a wire rack for 5 minutes. Transfer the cupcakes to the wire rack and let cool completely, about 1 hour.

Using a paring knife, cut a 1½-inch round piece about 1 inch deep from the center of each cupcake (see page 14). Fill each hollow with about 1 tablespoon warm chocolate glaze and chill until the filling is set, about 10 minutes. Frost the cupcakes with the buttercream and serve. (The filled and frosted cupcakes can be refrigerated in an airtight container for up to 3 days; bring to room temperature before serving.)

Black & White Cupcakes

These cupcakes, a divine combination of chocolate cake and cheesecake, are ooey-gooey delicious. They're best eaten the day they are made, but if you happen to have leftovers, they can be gently reheated before serving.

8 oz cream cheese, at room temperature

1 tbsp sour cream

1¼ cups sugar

1 cup cake flour

⅓ cup unsweetened cocoa powder

½ tsp baking soda

¼ tsp salt

4 tbsp unsalted butter, at room temperature

1 large egg, at room temperature

1 tsp vanilla extract

½ cup whole milk

Gooey Chocolate Glaze (page 113)

Chocolate curls (see page 19) for garnish, optional

MAKES 12 CUPCAKES

Position a rack in the middle of the oven and preheat to 350°F. Lightly spray a standard 12-cup muffin pan with nonstick cooking spray. To make the cream cheese filling, in a bowl, using an electric mixer on high speed, beat the cream cheese until fluffy, about 2 minutes. Add the sour cream and ½ cup of the sugar and beat until combined.

To make the cupcake batter, sift together the cake flour, cocoa powder, baking soda, and salt into a bowl. In another bowl, using an electric mixer on medium-high speed, beat the butter and remaining ¾ cup sugar together until light and fluffy, 2–3 minutes. Add the egg and vanilla and beat until combined. Add the flour mixture in 3 additions, alternating with the milk in 2 additions, beating on low speed until just combined; scrape down the sides of the bowl as needed.

Divide the batter evenly among the prepared muffin cups, filling each about one-half full. Spoon the cream cheese filling onto the center of each, dividing it evenly (the filling will sink into the cupcakes as they bake). Bake until the cupcakes are set in the center, about 15 minutes. Let the cupcakes cool in the pan on a wire rack for 5 minutes. Transfer the cupcakes to the wire rack and let cool completely, about 1 hour.

Spoon the glaze over the cupcakes, top with chocolate curls, if using, and serve. (The finished cupcakes can be refrigerated in an airtight container for up to 3 days; reheat in a 250°F oven for 5 minutes before serving.)

Rocky Road Cupcakes

Chocolate, nuts, and marshmallows are the tasty trio that make up rocky road. These cupcakes call for walnuts, but just about any type of nut can be used in their place. A billowy frosting made with marshallows stands in for the marshmallows themselves.

Batter for Chocolate Cupcakes (page 27)

2 cups walnut halves, toasted (see page 8) and coarsely chopped

Marshmallow Frosting (page 109)

MAKES 12 CUPCAKES

Position a rack in the middle of the oven and preheat to 350°F. Line a standard 12-cup muffin pan with paper or foil liners.

Prepare the cupcake batter as directed and then stir 1½ cups of chopped walnuts into the batter until combined. Divide the batter evenly among the prepared muffin cups, filling each about three-fourths full. Scatter the remaining chopped walnuts on top of the batter in each cup. Bake until a toothpick inserted into the center of a cupcake comes out with only a few moist crumbs attached, 22–24 minutes. Let the cupcakes cool in the pan on a wire rack for 5 minutes. Transfer the cupcakes to the wire rack and let cool completely, about 1 hour.

Frost the cupcakes with the marshmallow frosting and serve. (The frosted cupcakes can be refrigerated in an airtight container for up to 4 days; bring to room temperature before serving.)

White Chocolate & Raspberry Cupcakes

Tart fresh raspberries are the perfect counterpoint to the sweetness of white chocolate. Don't worry if the raspberry juices run down the sides of the cupcakes—the color adds to the cupcakes' charm. Once they're frosted, serve the cupcakes without further ado.

1¼ cups cake flour

1 tsp baking powder

¼ tsp salt

¾ cup sugar

4 tbsp unsalted butter, at room temperature

1 large egg, at room temperature

½ cup whole milk

3 oz white chocolate, chopped

1 cup raspberries

White Chocolate Buttercream (page 105)

White chocolate curls (see page 19) for garnish, optional

MAKES 12 CUPCAKES

Position a rack in the middle of the oven and preheat to 350°F. Line a standard 12-cup muffin pan with paper or foil liners.

Sift together the flour, baking powder, and salt into a bowl. Using an electric mixer on medium-high speed, beat the sugar and butter together until light and fluffy, 2–3 minutes. Add the egg and beat until combined. Add the flour mixture in 3 additions, alternating with the milk in 2 additions, beating on low speed until combined; scrape down the sides of the bowl as needed. Add the white chocolate and beat on low speed until just combined.

Divide the batter evenly among the prepared muffin cups, filling each about three-fourths full. Bake until lightly golden and a toothpick inserted into the center of a cupcake comes out clean, 18–20 minutes. Let the cupcakes cool completely in the pan on a wire rack, about 1 hour. Remove the cupcakes from the pan. (The cooled cupcakes can be refrigerated in an airtight container for up to 3 days; bring the cupcakes to room temperature before finishing.)

Place the raspberries in a small bowl and use a fork to crush them lightly. Spoon the crushed raspberries on top of the cupcakes, dividing them evenly. Frost the cupcakes with the buttercream, garnish with white chocolate curls, if using, and serve right away.

Special-Occasion Cupcakes

Salted Caramel Cupcakes

These striking cupcakes feature an intriguing interplay of sweet and salty flavors. For an extra special touch, dip the bottoms of the caramel candies that will be used as garnishes into melted chocolate and let the chocolate cool before topping the cupcakes.

1¼ cups all-purpose flour

¾ tsp baking powder

¼ tsp salt

1 cup firmly packed dark brown sugar

½ cup granulated sugar

½ cup unsalted butter, at room temperature

2 large eggs, at room temperature

1 tsp vanilla extract

½ cup whole milk

Caramel Swirl Buttercream (page 105)

12 caramel candies

Sea salt

MAKES 12 CUPCAKES

Position a rack in the middle of the oven and preheat to 350°F. Line a standard 12-cup muffin pan with paper or foil liners.

In a bowl, whisk together the flour, baking powder and salt. In another bowl, using an electric mixer on medium-high speed, beat the sugars and butter together until light and fluffy, 2–3 minutes. Add the eggs and vanilla and beat until combined. Add flour mixture in 3 additions, alternating with the milk in 2 additions, beating on low speed until just combined; scrape down the sides of the bowl as needed.

Divide the batter evenly among the prepared muffin cups, filling each about two-thirds full. Bake until a toothpick inserted in the center of a cupcake comes out clean, 20–22 minutes. Let the cupcakes cool in the pan on a wire rack for 5 minutes. Transfer the cupcakes to the wire rack and let cool completely, about 1 hour.

Frost the cupcakes with the buttercream. (The frosted cupcakes can be refrigerated in an airtight container for up to 3 days; bring to room temperature before finishing.) Top each cupcake with a caramel candy, sprinkle with a pinch of sea salt, and serve.

Tres Leches Cupcakes

Tres leches means "three milks" in Spanish. It's a favorite Latin American dessert of light, airy cake soaked with evaporated milk, sweetened condensed milk, and heavy cream. This cupcake version is spiked with rum for a little extra kick.

1 can (12 oz) sweetened condensed milk

1 can (12 oz) evaporated milk

1 cup heavy cream

¼ cup dark rum

1 cup all-purpose flour

¾ cup sugar

1 tsp baking powder

¼ tsp salt

3 large eggs, at room temperature

½ cup whole milk

1 tsp vanilla extract

Sweetened Whipped Cream (page 110)

MAKES 12 CUPCAKES

Position a rack in the middle of the oven and preheat to 350°F. Line a standard 12-cup muffin pan with paper or foil liners. In a bowl, stir together the sweetened condensed milk, evaporated milk, heavy cream, and rum.

In a medium bowl, whisk together the flour, sugar, baking powder, and salt. Add the eggs, milk, and vanilla, whisking vigorously to combine.

Divide the batter among the prepared muffin cups, filling each about two-thirds full. Bake until lightly golden and a toothpick inserted in the center of a cupcake comes out clean, 18–20 minutes. Transfer the pan to a wire rack. While the cupcakes are still hot and in the muffin pan, carefully pierce the top of each cupcake several times with a toothpick. Spoon the sweetened condensed milk mixture generously over each cupcake, dividing it evenly. Let the soaked cupcakes cool completely in the pan, about 1 hour.

Transfer the cupcakes to an airtight container and chill for at least 4 hours or for up to 3 days. Let the cupcakes stand at room temperature for about 10 minutes, then frost with the whipped cream and serve right away.

Tiramisu Cupcakes

Refrigerating these decadent cupcakes for up to 4 days before serving gives the flavors a chance to meld. The liqueur–based soaking liquid also has time to work its way throughout the cupcakes, making them ultra–moist, flavorful, and indulgent.

Yellow Cupcakes (page 24)

½ **cup strong brewed coffee, at room temperature**

¼ **cup dark rum**

½ **cup Kahlúa or other coffee-flavored liqueur**

2 **tbsp Amaretto or other almond-flavored liqueur**

1 **lb mascarpone cheese**

1 **cup heavy cream**

¼ **cup confectioners' sugar**

1 **tsp vanilla extract**

1 **oz semisweet chocolate, grated**

MAKES 12 CUPCAKES

Bake and cool the cupcakes according to the recipe and set aside.

In a small bowl, stir together the coffee, rum, ¼ cup of the Kahlúa, and the Amaretto. In a bowl, with an electric mixer on medium-low speed, beat the mascarpone, heavy cream, sugar, vanilla, and the remaining ¼ cup Kahlúa until just combined; do not overmix.

Brush the cooled cupcakes generously with the coffee mixture, dividing it evenly. Frost the cupcakes with the mascarpone mixture and sprinkle with the grated chocolate. Refrigerate the cupcakes in an airtight container for at least 4 hours or for up to 4 days. Let the cupcakes stand at room temperature for 10–15 minutes before serving.

Jumbo Malted Chocolate Chip Cupcakes

With a candy garnish and chocolate-speckled interior, these oversized kid-pleasing cupcakes are perfect for those with a serious sweet tooth. If you can't find liners to fit the jumbo muffin pan, simply spray the pan with nonstick cooking spray.

1⅔ cups all-purpose flour

⅔ cup malted milk powder

½ cup granulated sugar

¼ cup firmly packed light brown sugar

2 tsp baking powder

¼ tsp salt

½ cup whole milk

6 tbsp unsalted butter, melted

2 large eggs, at room temperature

1 tsp vanilla extract

4 oz semisweet chocolate, finely chopped

Chocolate Malt Buttercream (page 105)

Chocolate malt ball candies, coarsely chopped, for garnish, optional

MAKES 6 JUMBO CUPCAKES

Position a rack in the middle of the oven and preheat to 350°F. Line a 6-cup jumbo muffin pan with jumbo liners.

In a bowl, whisk together the flour, malted milk powder, granulated sugar, brown sugar, baking powder, and salt. In a small bowl, whisk together the milk, melted butter, eggs, and vanilla. Add the milk mixture to the flour mixture. Using an electric mixer on medium speed, beat until just combined; scrape down the sides of the bowl as needed. Stir in the chopped chocolate.

Divide the batter evenly among the prepared muffin cups, filling each about one-half full. Bake until lightly golden and a toothpick inserted in the center of a cupcake comes out clean, 25–28 minutes. Let the cupcakes cool in the pan on a wire rack for 5 minutes. Transfer the cupcakes to the wire rack and let cool completely, about 1 hour.

Frost the cupcakes with the buttercream. (The frosted cupcakes can be refrigerated in an airtight container for up to 3 days; bring to room temperature before finishing.) Top with the chopped chocolate malt ball candies, if using, and serve.

Mini Sticky Toffee Pudding Cupcakes

These may be mini cupcakes, but they are big on sweet, rich, nutty flavor. The sticky toffee topping is indeed sticky, so it's best to eat these cupcakes with a fork even though they are bite-sized, or serve them with lots of napkins.

1 cup pitted dates, coarsely chopped

1 tsp vanilla extract

¾ tsp baking soda

¾ cup boiling water

1½ cups all-purpose flour

2 tsp baking powder

¼ tsp salt

½ cup plus 6 tbsp unsalted butter, at room temperature

¾ cup granulated sugar

2 large eggs, at room temperature

½ cup pecans, toasted (see page 8) and coarsely chopped

1 cup firmly packed light brown sugar

6 tbsp heavy cream

MAKES 24 MINI CUPCAKES

Position a rack in the middle of the oven and preheat to 350°F. Lightly spray a 24-cup miniature muffin pan with nonstick cooking spray.

In a small bowl, combine the dates, vanilla, and baking soda. Pour the boiling water over the dates and let cool to room temperature. In a bowl, whisk together the flour, baking powder, and salt. In another bowl, with an electric mixer on medium-high speed, beat the 6 tablespoons butter and granulated sugar until light and fluffy, 2–3 minutes. Add the eggs and beat to combine. Add the flour mixture and beat on low speed until just combined; scrape down the sides of the bowl as needed. Stir in the date mixture.

Divide the batter evenly among the prepared muffin cups, filling them about two-thirds full. Bake until golden brown and just set in the center, 12–15 minutes. Let the cupcakes cool in the pan on a wire rack for 5 minutes. Transfer the cupcakes to the rack and let cool 10–15 minutes. (The cooled cupcakes can be refrigerated in an airtight container for up to 3 days; reheat in a 250°F oven for about 10 minutes before finishing.)

While the cupcakes are still warm, in a saucepan over medium-high heat, combine the pecans, brown sugar, and cream. Cook, stirring occasionally, until the sugar dissolves. Spoon the warm pecan mixture over the warm cupcakes and serve right away.

Ice Cream Cupcakes

If the cookies cool down and become brittle before you can form them into cups, simply return them to the oven for a few minutes until they're once again soft and pliable. If the cookie cups break, use the leftover dough to bake and shape more cups.

FOR THE COOKIE CUPS

4 tbsp unsalted butter

¼ cup light corn syrup

¼ cup sugar

¼ cup all-purpose flour

Pinch salt

Batter for Vanilla Cupcakes (page 23)

1 quart ice cream or sherbet, such as raspberry or chocolate, slightly softened

Colored sugar for garnish, optional

MAKES 12 CUPCAKES

Position a rack in the middle of the oven and preheat to 350°F. Line 3 large cookie sheets with parchment paper. To make the cookie cups, in a saucepan over medium heat, combine the butter, corn syrup, and sugar and bring to a boil, stirring occasionally, until the sugar dissolves. Remove from the heat and whisk in the flour and salt until combined. Let cool completely, about 30 minutes. Scoop up a rounded teaspoon of dough and place it on a prepared cookie sheet. Repeat until you have 4 evenly spaced dough portions per cookie sheet (you will have leftover dough). Bake the cookies 1 sheet at a time until golden, about 10 minutes. Let cool until the edges set, 1–2 minutes. Right away, use a small offset spatula to carefully lift off each cookie, then fit the cookie into a muffin pan cup, gently pressing it into the sides. Let the cookie cups cool to room temperature, then remove them from the pan.

Spray the muffin pan with nonstick cooking spray. Divide the cupcake batter evenly among the prepared muffin pan cups, filling them about three-fourths full. Bake until golden and a toothpick inserted into the center of a cupcake comes out clean, 18–20 minutes. Let the cupcakes cool in the pan on a wire rack for 5 minutes. Transfer the cupcakes to the wire rack and let cool completely, about 1 hour.

When ready to serve, place a cupcake into each cookie cup, trimming it to fit, if needed, and top with a scoop of ice cream. Sprinkle with colored sugar, if using, and serve right away.

Easter Egg Nest Cupcakes

Toasting the coconut that forms the nests adds a natural straw color as well as a pleasant crunch and nutty flavor to these whimsical cupcakes. Easter egg candies come in many different sizes; use as many as will comfortably fit in each nest.

¾ cup sweetened shredded coconut

1¼ cups all-purpose flour

1¼ tsp baking powder

¼ tsp salt

¼ cup sour cream

2 tbsp vegetable oil

½ tsp vanilla extract

¾ cup sugar

6 tbsp unsalted butter, at room temperature

2 large eggs, at room temperature

Almond Buttercream (page 105)

Easter egg candies

MAKES 12 CUPCAKES

Position a rack in the middle of the oven and preheat to 350°F. Spread the coconut on a baking sheet and toast until lightly browned, about 8 minutes. Line a standard 12-cup muffin pan with paper or foil liners.

In a large bowl, whisk together the flour, baking powder and salt. In a small bowl, stir together the sour cream, oil, and vanilla. In another bowl, with an electric mixer on medium-high speed, beat the sugar and butter together until light and fluffy, 2–3 minutes. Add the eggs, one at a time, beating well after each addition. Add the flour mixture in 3 additions, alternating with the sour cream mixture in 2 additions, beating on low speed until just combined; scrape down the sides of the bowl as needed.

Divide the batter evenly among the prepared muffin cups, filling each about three-fourths full. Bake until lightly golden on top and a toothpick inserted in the center of a cupcake comes out clean, 18–20 minutes. Let the cupcakes cool in the pan on a wire rack for 5 minutes. Transfer the cupcakes to the wire rack and let cool completely, about 1 hour.

Frost the cupcakes with the buttercream. Top each cupcake with a ring of toasted coconut. Place an Easter egg candy (or candies) in the center of each nest and serve. (The finished cupcakes can be refrigerated in an airtight container for up to 2 days; bring the cupcakes to room temperature before serving.)

Fourth of July Cupcakes

Fresh currants, sparkling with jewel-like color, are a beautiful way to decorate these cupcakes in red, white, and blue, and star-shaped sprinkles add a celebratory feel. For a fun, festive look, bake the cupcakes in liners that boast a Fourth of July theme.

Vanilla Cupcakes (page 23)

Cream Cheese Frosting (page 106)

½ **cup red currants (see note)**

½ **cup white currants (see note)**

½ **cup black currants (see note)**

Star-shaped sprinkles for garnish, optional

MAKES 12 CUPCAKES

Bake and cool the cupcakes according to the recipe.

Frost the cupcakes with the cream cheese frosting. For piping techniques, see pages 16–17. (The frosted cupcakes can be refrigerated in an airtight container for up to 2 days; bring to room temperature before finishing.) Top each cupcake with an assortment of currants, dividing them evenly. Garnish the cupcakes, cupcake platter, or individual cupcake plates with star-shaped sprinkles, if using, and serve.

Note Currants are often available in farmers' markets and specialty grocery stores. They are in season in the summer, just in time for Fourth of July celebrations. If you cannot find them, feel free to substitute strawberries, raspberries, and blueberries.

Creepy Crawler Halloween Cupcakes

Devil's Food Cupcakes are a fitting base for these Halloween cupcakes with a spider web design. For a fun, festive touch, the icing for making the spider webs can be tinted light orange with food coloring paste (for more information on food coloring, see page 9).

**Devil's Food Cupcakes
(page 28; omit the Rich
Chocolate Glaze)**

FOR THE MILK
CHOCOLATE GLAZE

½ **cup heavy cream**

1 tbsp light corn syrup

Pinch salt

**8 oz milk chocolate,
chopped**

Vanilla Glaze (page 114)

**12 gummy or licorice spiders
(see note)**

MAKES 12 CUPCAKES

Bake and cool the cupcakes according to the recipe.

To make the glaze, in a small saucepan over medium-high heat, combine the cream, corn syrup, and salt and bring to a simmer. Remove from heat and add the chocolate; let stand for 3 minutes. Using a rubber spatula, stir until the chocolate is melted and the mixture is smooth. Transfer the chocolate glaze to a small bowl and let cool to room temperature, about 15 minutes.

Place the vanilla glaze in a parchment paper cone or small pastry bag fitted with a fine writing tip.

Spoon the chocolate glaze over the cupcakes. Using the vanilla glaze, create spider web designs on top of each cupcake (see page 18). (The glazed cupcakes can be refrigerated in an airtight container for up to 3 days; bring to room temperature before finishing.) Arrange the spiders on or around the cupcakes and serve.

Note You can use gummy spiders to decorate the cupcakes, but for a more realistic—and creepier—look, make your own spiders out of licorice candies. Cut 36 one-inch lengths of black licorice laces, then halve each piece lengthwise. Using a wooden skewer, poke 3 holes on each side of 12 licorice drops, then insert a licorice lace piece into each hole.

Christmas Peppermint Cupcakes

Crushed peppermint candy peeks out from under the frosting of these winter-themed cupcakes. Using green candy along with some red adds a splash of holiday color. Pipe the frosting with festive flair to give the cupcakes a look to match the season.

1¼ cups all-purpose flour

1¼ tsp baking powder

¼ tsp salt

1 cup sugar

6 tbsp unsalted butter, at room temperature

1 large egg plus 1 large egg white, at room temperature

1 tsp peppermint extract

½ cup whole milk

Basic Buttercream (page 104)

¾ cup crushed peppermint candies

MAKES 12 CUPCAKES

Position a rack in the middle of the oven and preheat to 350°F. Line a standard 12-cup muffin pan with paper or foil liners.

In a bowl, whisk together the flour, baking powder, and salt. In another bowl, with an electric mixer on medium-high speed, beat the sugar and butter together until light and fluffy, 2–3 minutes. Add the egg, egg white, and ½ teaspon of peppermint extract and beat until combined. Add the flour mixture in 3 additions, alternating with the milk in 2 additions, beating on low speed until just combined; scrape down the sides of the bowl as needed.

Divide the batter evenly among the prepared muffin cups, filling each about three-fourths full. Bake until lightly golden and a toothpick inserted in the center of a cupcake comes out clean, 18–20 minutes. Let the cupcakes cool in the pan on a wire rack for 5 minutes. Transfer the cupcakes to the wire rack and let cool completely, about 1 hour. (The cooled cupcakes can be refrigerated in an airtight container for up to 3 days; bring to room temperature before finishing.)

Whisk the reamining ½ teaspoon of peppermint extract into the Basic Buttercream until combined. Top the cooled cupcakes with the peppermint candy, frost with the buttercream, and serve.

Frostings, Fillings & Finishes

Basic Buttercream

This rich, not-too-sweet buttercream can be made (with flavorings) in advance and refrigerated in an airtight container for up to 5 days. Before using the buttercream, bring it to room temperature and beat it on medium-low speed until smooth.

3 large egg whites, at room temperature

¾ cup sugar

Pinch salt

1 cup unsalted butter, cut into 16 pieces, at room temperature

Flavoring(s) of choice (right)

MAKES ABOUT 2 CUPS

In a large, clean heatproof bowl, combine the egg whites and sugar. Set the bowl over (but not touching) simmering water in a saucepan and heat the mixture, whisking constantly, until the sugar has completely dissolved and the mixture is very warm to the touch (about 160°F on an instant-read thermometer), about 2 minutes. Remove the bowl from the saucepan. Using an electric mixer on high speed, beat the egg white mixture until it is fluffy, cooled to room temperature, and holds stiff peaks (the mixture should not look dry), about 6 minutes.

With the mixer on medium-low speed, add the salt and the butter, a few pieces at a time, beating well after each addition. If the frosting appears to separate or is very liquid after all the butter is added, continue to beat on high speed until it is smooth and creamy, 3–5 minutes more. Add the flavoring(s) of choice and beat until combined, scraping down the sides of the bowl as needed. Use right away.

Buttercream Flavors

To make any of these buttercream flavors, follow the recipe for Basic Buttercream (left) to make the base, then add the desired flavorings at the very end, once all the butter has been incorporated, and mix until thoroughly combined.

Almond Buttercream ½ tsp vanilla extract and ¼ tsp almond extract

Banana Buttercream 2 ripe bananas mashed with 2 tbsp sour cream until smooth

Caramel Swirl Buttercream 1 recipe Caramel Drizzle (page 116; mix only until swirled)

Chocolate Buttercream 2 tbsp unsweetened cocoa powder whisked into 4 oz semisweet chocolate, melted and slightly cooled (see page 70)

Chocolate Malt Buttercream 2 tbsp unsweetened cocoa powder whisked into 4 oz semisweet chocolate, melted and slightly cooled (see page 70); and ¼ cup malted milk powder whisked into ¼ cup milk until dissolved

Chocolate-Mint Buttercream ½ tsp peppermint extract and 2 tbsp unsweetened cocoa powder whisked into 4 oz semisweet chocolate, melted and slightly cooled (see page 70)

Coconut Buttercream ½ tsp coconut extract

Coffee Buttercream ½ cup strong brewed coffee, at room temperature

Rum Buttercream 1½ tbsp dark rum

Strawberry Buttercream ⅓ cup strained strawberry preserves and 6 drops red food coloring

Vanilla Buttercream seeds from ½ vanilla bean and/or 1 tsp vanilla extract

White Chocolate Buttercream 4 oz white chocolate, melted and slightly cooled (see page 70)

... Cream Cheese Frosting

Sweet, slightly tangy cream cheese frosting is easy to make, and its versatile flavor pairs well with many different types of cupcakes. Sifting the confectioners' sugar removes lumps, so for a silky smooth frosting, don't skip this step.

12 oz cream cheese, at room temperature

6 tbsp unsalted butter, at room temperature

½ tsp vanilla extract

1 cup confectioners' sugar, sifted

MAKES ABOUT 2 CUPS

In a bowl, with an electric mixer on medium-high speed, beat the cream cheese, butter, and vanilla together until light and fluffy, about 2 minutes. Gradually beat in the sugar and mix until thoroughly combined; scrape down the sides of the bowl as needed. Use right away, or if the consistency is too soft, refrigerate until the frosting is spreadable, about 15 minutes.

Cream Cheese Frosting with Buttered Pecans Toast ½ cup pecans (see page 8) and let cool completely. Coarsely chop the pecans and transfer to a small bowl. In a small saucepan, heat 4 tablespoons unsalted butter over medium-low heat, whisking frequently, until fragrant and nutty brown, 3–4 minutes. Pour the brown butter over the chopped pecans, add a pinch of salt, and toss to coat; set aside to cool to room temperature. Follow the recipe for Cream Cheese Frosting, stirring the cooled buttered pecans into the finished frosting until combined.

Honey–Cream Cheese Frosting Follow the recipe for Cream Cheese Frosting, reducing the confectioners' sugar to ½ cup. Add 2 tablespoons honey along with the confectioners' sugar.

Peanut Butter Frosting

If you thought peanut butter couldn't get any better, try this super-simple frosting. For the richest peanut flavor, use natural or old-fashioned peanut butter, but before using it, make sure that it has been stirred well and is not at all separated.

6 tbsp unsalted butter, at room temperature

¾ cup confectioners' sugar, sifted

¾ cup smooth peanut butter

¼ cup heavy cream

MAKES ABOUT 1½ CUPS

In a bowl, with an electric mixer on medium-low speed, beat the butter, sugar, peanut butter, and cream together until smooth and combined, about 2 minutes; scrape down the sides of the bowl as needed. Use right away. (The frosting can be stored in an airtight container for up to 4 days; bring to room temperature before using.)

Meringue Frosting

This glossy white, light-as-air frosting can be formed into dramatic peaks and curls for decoration, and it can be lightly browned with a kitchen torch once it has topped the cupcakes. It doesn't hold well, so be prepared to use it right away.

3 large egg whites

¾ cup sugar

2 tbsp water

1 tbsp light corn syrup

½ tsp vanilla extract

MAKES ABOUT 4 CUPS

In a large, clean heatproof bowl, combine the egg whites, sugar, water, and corn syrup. Set the bowl over (but not touching) simmering water in a saucepan and heat the mixture, whisking constantly, until the sugar has dissolved and the mixture is very warm to the touch (about 160°F on an instant-read thermometer), about 2 minutes. Remove the bowl from the saucepan. Using an electric mixer on high speed, beat the mixture until glossy and voluminous, about 5 minutes. Beat in the vanilla. Use right away.

Marshmallow Frosting

For a smooth, fluffy frosting, make sure that the sugar dissolves completely while the egg white mixture is whisked over the heat. And make sure that the mixture is still very warm when you add the marshmallows so that the marshallows will fully melt.

2 large egg whites

1 cup sugar

6 tbsp water

1 tbsp light corn syrup

½ tsp cream of tartar

Pinch salt

1 cup miniature marshmallows

1 tsp vanilla extract

MAKES 5 CUPS

In a large, clean heatproof bowl, combine the egg whites, sugar, water, corn syrup, cream of tartar, and salt. Set the bowl over (but not touching) simmering water in a saucepan and heat the mixture, whisking constantly, until the sugar has dissolved and the mixture is very warm to the touch (about 160°F on an instant-read thermometer), about 2 minutes. Remove the bowl from the saucepan. Using an electric mixer on medium-high speed, beat the mixture until it is very warm and soft (but not dry) peaks form, about 2 minutes. Reduce the mixer to low and add the marshmallows and vanilla. Continue beating until the marshmallows are melted and the frosting is completely smooth, about 2 minutes more. Use right away.

Sweetened Whipped Cream

Sweetened whipped cream is the perfect accompaniment to desserts of all kinds and is an easy topping for cupcakes. If you use a chilled bowl and beaters to whip the cream, the cream will whip up quickly and with lots of volume.

1 cup cold heavy cream

2 tbsp confectioners' sugar

MAKES ABOUT 1½ CUPS

In a chilled bowl, combine the cream and sugar. Using an electric mixer on low speed, beat until slightly thickened, 1–2 minutes. Gradually increase the speed to medium-high and continue to beat until the cream holds soft peaks, 2–3 minutes. Use right away.

Honey Whipped Cream Follow the recipe for Sweetened Whipped Cream, replacing the confectioners' sugar with 2 tablespoons honey.

German Chocolate Topping

This topping, a necessary part, and arguably the best part, of any German chocolate cake or cupcake, does double duty as a filling. It combines the chewiness of shredded coconut, the crispness of toasted pecans, and the richness of butter.

¾ cup evaporated milk

½ cup firmly packed light brown sugar

½ cup unsalted butter, cut into 8 pieces

1⅓ cup sweetened shredded coconut

1 cup pecans, toasted (see page 8) and coarsely chopped

Pinch salt

MAKES ABOUT 3 CUPS

In a small saucepan over medium-high heat, combine the evaporated milk, brown sugar, and butter and bring to a simmer, stirring occasionally. Remove the pan from the heat. Stir in the coconut, pecans, and salt until combined. Let cool to room temperature before using.

Rich Chocolate Glaze

This smooth, shiny, very chocolaty glaze can be used as a cupcake filling or as a cupcake topping alone or under another type frosting. For the deepest, most complex chocolate flavor, opt for the best-quality semisweet chocolate you can find.

1 cup heavy cream

1 tbsp light corn syrup

Pinch salt

8 oz semisweet chocolate, chopped

MAKES ABOUT 1¾ CUPS

In a small saucepan combine the cream, corn syrup, and salt. Bring to a simmer over medium-high heat. Remove the pan from the heat, add the chocolate, and let stand for about 3 minutes. Using a wooden spoon, stir the mixture until the chocolate is completely melted and the mixture is smooth. Let cool to room temperature and use right away. (The cooled glaze can be refrigerated in an airtight container for up to 3 days; before using, soften the glaze by gently heating it in a heatproof bowl set over, but not touching, simmering water in a saucepan.)

Gooey Chocolate Glaze

The sweetened condensed milk in this glaze makes it sweeter and stickier than the Rich Chocolate Glaze (left). Be sure to use regular sweetened condensed milk, not the nonfat or low-fat versions which will affect the flavor and texture of the glaze.

⅔ **cup sweetened condensed milk**

8 oz semisweet chocolate, chopped

2 tbsp unsalted butter, cut into 2 pieces

MAKES ABOUT 1½ CUPS

In a small saucepan, combine the sweetened condensed milk, chocolate, and butter. Warm the mixture over medium-high heat, stirring occasionally, until the chocolate is melted and the mixture is bubbly, 3–4 minutes. Remove the pan from the heat and let the glaze cool slightly before using. (The cooled glaze can be refrigerated in an airtight container for up to 5 days; before using, soften the glaze by gently heating it in a heatproof bowl set over, but not touching, simmering water in a saucepan.)

Vanilla Glaze

The seeds from half of a vanilla bean can be added to this glaze to give it extra-rich vanilla flavor and fragrance, as well as visual appeal. The glaze and any of its variations dries and hardens slightly upon standing, so be sure to use it as soon as you make it.

1 cup confectioners' sugar, plus more as needed

2 tbsp whole milk, plus more as needed

1 tsp vanilla extract

MAKES ABOUT 1 CUP

In a bowl, whisk together the sugar, milk, and vanilla until smooth; the glaze should be spreadable. If it seems too thick, whisk in additional milk a few drops at a time; if it seems too thin, whisk in additional sugar one teaspoon at a time. Use right away.

Lemon Glaze Follow the recipe for Vanilla Glaze, replacing the milk with fresh lemon juice and the vanilla with 2 teaspoons finely grated lemon zest.

Maple Glaze Follow the recipe for Vanilla Glaze, reducing the milk to 1 tablespoon and replacing the vanilla with 2 teaspoons maple extract.

Rose Water Glaze Follow the recipe for Vanilla Glaze, reducing the milk to 1 tablespoon, replacing the vanilla with 1 teaspoon rose water, and adding 2 drops red food coloring.

Tangerine Glaze Follow the recipe for Vanilla Glaze, replacing the milk with freshly squeezed tangerine juice and the vanilla with 2 teaspoons finely grated tangerine zest.

Grapefruit or Lime Curd ● ● ● ● ● ● ● ● ● ● ● ● ● ● ●

If you're making grapefruit curd, use ruby grapefruit for its beautiful pinkish color. When grating the zest, be sure to remove only the colored part of the peel where the flavorful oils reside, not any of the bitter white pith that is just underneath.

6 tbsp fresh grapefruit or lime juice

½ **cup sugar**

4 large egg yolks

Pinch salt

4 tbsp unsalted butter, cut into 4 pieces

2 tsp finely grated grapefruit or lime zest

MAKES 1 CUP

In a heavy-bottomed nonreactive saucepan, whisk together the grapefruit or lime juice, sugar, egg yolks, and salt. Cook the mixture over medium-high heat, whisking constantly and scraping the sides of the pan, until the curd is thick enough to coat the back of a spoon, 5–8 minutes; do not let the curd boil (if it is allowed to boil, it will turn lumpy).

Remove the saucepan from the heat. Whisk in the butter, one piece at a time, until smooth. Strain the curd through a fine-mesh sieve into a bowl. Stir in the grapefruit or lime zest and cover with plastic wrap, pressing it directly onto the surface of the curd to prevent a skin from forming. Refrigerate until chilled and set, at least 1 hour or for up to 3 days.

Caramel Drizzle

A drizzle of thick, rich, bittersweet caramel makes even the most mundane of cupcakes special. When cooking the caramel, once it begins to take on color, keep a close watch because it darkens very quickly. The darker the caramel, the more bitter it will be.

1½ cups sugar

1¼ cups heavy cream

Pinch salt

MAKES ABOUT 2½ CUPS

In a heavy-bottomed, high-sided saucepan, cook the sugar over medium-high heat until it begins to melt around the edges, about 5 minutes. Stirring with a clean wooden spoon, continue to cook until the sugar is melted and has turned golden amber, about 3 minutes longer.

Carefully pour the cream down the side of the pan in a slow, steady stream (it will bubble and spatter), stirring constantly until completely smooth. Stir in the salt. Pour the caramel into a small heatproof bowl and let cool completely before using. (The caramel can be stored in an airtight container in the refrigerator for up to 1 week; bring to room temperature before using.)

Candied Grapefruit Peel

Ruby grapefruit, with its pinkish hue, makes beautiful candied peel, but any type of grapefruit will do. This method can also be used to make candied lemon, lime, or orange peel (use about 3 lemons or limes, or 2 oranges).

1 ruby grapefruit

3 cups sugar

MAKES ABOUT 24 PIECES

Cut the grapefruit into quarters and pull the flesh away from the pith and peel; reserve the flesh for another use. Cut the peel with the pith attached into ½-inch-wide strips.

Bring a saucepan three-fourths full of water to a boil over high heat. Add the grapefruit peel and boil for 4 minutes. Drain the peel and rinse under cold water. Repeat this step twice, using fresh water each time, to remove bitterness from the peel.

In a saucepan, combine 2 cups of the sugar, 1½ cups water, and the prepared grapefruit peel. Bring to a simmer over medium-low heat and cook until the peel is soft and translucent, about 30 minutes. Remove from the heat and let the peel cool to room temperature in the syrup.

Using a slotted spoon or tongs, transfer the grapefruit peel to a wire rack set over a rimmed baking sheet; discard the syrup. Let the peel stand until it is no longer wet and feels only slightly tacky to the touch, about 2 hours.

Spread the remaining 1 cup sugar in a shallow dish. Toss the peel in the sugar until all pieces are completely coated. Transfer to a clean wire rack and let dry for 1 hour. (The candied peel can be stored in an airtight container at room temperature for up to 5 days.)

Sugared Flowers & Petals

Look for organic edible flowers that have not been sprayed with pesticides, and make sure that the flowers are completely dry before you brush them. Two tablespoons of pasteurized egg whites can be used in place of the raw egg white if you prefer.

1 large egg white

24 organic edible flowers or petals, such as violets, pansies, and rose petals

1 cup superfine sugar

MAKES 24 SUGARED FLOWERS OR PETALS

In a small bowl, whisk the egg white with a few drops of water until foamy. Using a small paintbrush, lightly coat each flower or petal completely with the egg white mixture.

Sprinkle the coated flowers or petals evenly with the sugar, covering them completely, and transfer to a parchment paper–lined baking sheet to dry, about 1 hour. (The sugared flowers and petals may be stored in an airtight container at room temperature for up to 1 hour.)

Candied Carrots

Candied carrots are a fun, colorful garnish for the Carrot Cake Cupcakes (page 31). You will need a carrot with its green top still attached. Look for bunched carrots with fresh, vibrant greens in well-stocked grocery stores and supermarkets.

1 carrot with green top

½ **cup sugar**

MAKES 12 CANDIED CARROTS

Trim the top from the carrot and reserve. Peel the carrot. Using the vegetable peeler, shave 12 long, wide carrot strips and set aside.

In a saucepan combine the sugar and ½ cup water to a boil and bring to a boil over medium-high heat, stirring occasionally. When the sugar is dissolved, add the carrot strips; reduce the heat to medium-low and simmer until the carrot strips are translucent, about 10 minutes. Let the carrot strips cool completely in the sugar syrup. (The carrots in syrup can be stored in an airtight container in the refrigerator for up to 4 days.)

When ready to use, remove the carrot strips from the syrup. Roll up a strip tightly at first, gradually loosening the roll, to form an elongated cone. Trim a tiny sprig from the carrot top and tuck it into the open end of the cone. Repeat with the remaining carrot strips.

Creative Cupcaking

This book contains recipes for cupcakes as complete packages: A cupcake is matched with a frosting or glaze, and, in some cases, a filling. But there's no reason to feel tied to these suggestions. Just about any type of cupcake can be filled with any kind of filling, topped with any sort of frosting, and garnished with a variety of embellishments. Here are some ideas for mixing and matching components to create unique cupcake combinations. Feel free, too, to experiment with your own combinations.

Coconut Haystack Cupcakes = Chocolate Cupcakes 27 + Coconut Buttercream 105 + toasted coconut garnish

Chocolate–Peanut Butter Cupcakes = Devil's Food Cupcakes 28 + Peanut Butter Frosting 107 + chopped peanut garnish

Turtle Cupcakes = Chocolate Cupcakes 27 + Rich Chocolate Glaze 112 + Caramel Buttercream 105 + toasted pecan garnish

Eggnog Cupcakes = Gingerbread Cupcakes 32 + Rum Buttercream 105 + freshly grated nutmeg garnish

S'mores Cupcakes = Chocolate Cupcakes 27 + Marshmallow Frosting 109 + graham cracker crumb garnish

Hot Fudge Cupcakes = Molten Chocolate Cupcakes 74 + vanilla ice cream + Sweetened Whipped Cream 110 + maraschino cherries

Dulce de Leche Cupcakes = Vanilla Cupcakes 23 + Caramel Buttercream 105 + Caramel Drizzle 116

Lemon Lover's Cupcakes = Lemon Poppy Seed Cupcakes 38 + lemon curd filling + Lemon Glaze 114 + candied lemon zest

Mint Chocolate Brownie Sundaes = Mini Chocolate-Mint Cupcakes 73 + vanilla ice cream + hot fudge sauce

Presenting your Cupcakes

Frosted cupcakes with decorations or garnishes require minimal effort to dress them up for serving. For casual gatherings, simply set the cupcakes on colorful napkins. For fancier affairs, place each cupcake on small a hors d'oeuvre plate or on a saucer of a color and shape that flatters the cupcakes' design. To present a grouping of cupcakes, arrange them on a large, flat tray or platter. For a grand presentation, arrange the cupcakes on a cake stand or on a tiered cupcake stand designed just for the purpose.

If you need to transport cupcakes, consider baking and frosting the cupcakes in advance and refrigerating them so that they're cold and firm, and therefore less likely to be damaged during travel. Set the cupcakes back in the muffin pan so that they are stable, then tent them with a large sheet of foil. As an extra precautionary measure, toothpicks can be inserted into each of the four corner cupcakes before tenting with foil. (The toothpicks will help prevent the foil from touching and marring the cupcakes' surfaces.) Another good option is a flat, wide container that's deeper than the cupcakes are high, like a cake or pie box from a bakery. Try to pack the cupcakes fairly tightly—too much space and they'll tip over. The best and safest option for transporting cupcakes, however, is a cupcake carrier with a solid lid and handles that will protect the cupcakes from any sort of in-transit damage.

Packing a single frosted cupcake for a lunchbox is always a conundrum. A single cupcake carrier offers the perfect solution, but a clean pint-size plastic deli container works as well. Set the cupcake on the overturned lid and cover with the inverted container, pressing it securely in place. The cupcake will be well protected, and since it's sitting on the lid, not inside the container, it's easy to remove. To pack a single cupcake as a gift, place it in a colorful Chinese-style take-out container, and, of course, embellish with a bow.

CUPCAKE BUFFET

A cupcake buffet is perfect for a casual party or dessert-time amusement for kids and adults alike. Bake a couple different kinds of basic cupcakes and leave them unfrosted. Whip up a few types and flavors of frostings and set them out in bowls, each with a butter knife or small icing spatula. Finally, set out a few options for garnishes—colorful sprinkles, chopped toasted nuts, shredded coconut, crushed toffee bits, shaved chocolate, fresh berries—and allow your guests to choose, frost, and decorate their own cupcakes to suit their own tastes.

Index

FIRESIDE
A Division of Simon & Schuster, Inc.
1230 Avenue of the Americas
New York, NY 10020

WELDON OWEN INC.

Chief Executive Officer, Weldon Owen Group John Owen
Chief Executive Officer & President, Weldon Owen Inc. Terry Newell
Chief Financial Officer Simon Fraser
Vice President Sales & New Business Development Amy Kaneko
Vice President and Creative Director Gaye Allen
Vice President and Publisher Hannah Rahill
Executive Editor Jennifer Newens
Senior Editor Dawn Yanagihara
Art Director Kara Church
Senior Designer Ashley Martinez
Designer Meghan Hildebrand
Production Director Chris Hemesath
Production Manager Michelle Duggan
Color Manager Teri Bell

Photographer David Matheson
Food Stylist Shelly Kaldunski

Manufactured in China
10 9 8 7 6 5 4 3 2

ISBN-13: 978-1-4165-8900-6
ISBN-10:   1-4165-8900-7

ACKNOWLEDGMENTS

Weldon Owen wishes to thank the following people for their generous support in producing this book:
Prop Stylist Daniele Maxwell; **Photographer's Assistant** Tony Jett; **Food Stylist's Assistant** Lillian Kang; **Copyeditor** Kate Washington;
Proofreader Lesli Neilson; **Indexer** Ken DellaPenta; **Recipe Consultant** Donita Boles; **Photo Consultant** Andrea Stephany